BRIGHT NOTES

REMEMBRANCE OF THINGS PAST BY MARCEL PROUST

Intelligent Education

INFLUENCE PUBLISHERS

Nashville, Tennessee

BRIGHT NOTES: Remembrance of Things Past
www.BrightNotes.com

No part of this publication may be used or reproduced in any manner whatsoever without written permission, except in the case of brief quotations in critical articles and reviews. For permissions, contact Influence Publishers http://www.influencepublishers.com.

ISBN: 978-1-645423-24-9 (Paperback)
ISBN: 978-1-645423-25-6 (eBook)

Published in accordance with the U.S. Copyright Office Orphan Works and Mass Digitization report of the register of copyrights, June 2015.

Originally published by Monarch Press.
Carolyn Roberts Welch, 1973
2020 Edition published by Influence Publishers.

Interior design by Lapiz Digital Services. Cover Design by Thinkpen Designs.

Printed in the United States of America.

Library of Congress Cataloging-in-Publication Data forthcoming.
Names: Intelligent Education
Title: BRIGHT NOTES: Remembrance of Things Past
Subject: STU004000 STUDY AIDS / Book Notes

CONTENTS

1)	Introduction to Marcel Proust	1
2)	Literary and Philosophical Influences on Marcel Proust	14
3)	Involuntary Memory	25
4)	Proust's Conception of Metaphor	28
5)	Basic Structure	30
6)	Significant Places	36
7)	The Seven Novels of Remembrance of Things Past	38
8)	Three Circles of Characters	114
9)	Proustian Artist-Figure as a Forgotten Man	124
10)	Analysis of Proust's Style	127
11)	Theme of Hidden Vice: Biblical Roots and its Emergence in Modern Literature	132

12)	Translation of Proust into English	135
13)	Recapitulation: Remembrance of Things Past as an Artistic Unity	141
14)	Essay Questions and Answers	146
15)	Bibliography	155

MARCEL PROUST

INTRODUCTION

GENERAL INTRODUCTION TO THE GROWTH OF PROUST'S REPUTATION

The fact that more has been written about Marcel Proust's *À la Recherche du temps perdu (Remembrance of Things Past)* than about any other twentieth-century work attests to the present reputation of its author. However, before he gained recognition for *À l'Ombre des jeunes filles en fleurs (Within a Budding Grove)* by winning the Goncourt Prize in 1918, at which time his earlier *Du Côté de chez Swann (Swann's Way)* likewise gained renown, Proust was regarded by many in literary circles as a mere dilettante. After *À l'Ombre des jeunes filles en fleurs*, Proust's reputation began to fluctuate. Even though his popularity and acclaim grew through *Le Côté de Guermantes (The Guermantes Way)*, it suffered with *Sodome et Gomorrhe (Cities of the Plain)* because this work was considered regressive by many. Even though *La Prisonnière (The Captive)* and *Albertine Disparue (The Sweet Cheat Gone)* were somewhat less depressing, they were still the work of a dying man and suffered from similar weaknesses. Sections from these works, however, do show Proust at his best. The response to *Le Temps retrouvé (The Past*

Recaptured) was highly favorable. Even though this work also contains some of Proust's best writing, much of the content is from the pre-World War I vintage which brought *Du Côté de chez Swann*.

The spread of Proust's reputation to the Anglo-Saxon world was launched by the London publisher Chatto and Windus, which published Charles Kenneth Scott-Moncrieff's superlative translation of the work, *Remembrance of Things Past*, up through the sixth novel, *The Sweet Cheat Gone*. *The Past Recaptured* was promptly set forth after the Sterlingshire Scotsman's death. The Scott-Moncrieff masterpiece was brought to the United States through the sense of preservation and literary vision of the late Bennett Cerf, president of Random House, who secured the rights not only to Proust's *Remembrance of Things Past* but to the masterpieces of other great Proust-influenced European authors, including James Joyce and Virginia Woolf.

PROUST'S CHILDHOOD AND YOUTH

Many of the biographical events of Marcel Proust's life pale as merely incidental when viewed in the light of the phenomenal *Remembrance of Things Past*. Nevertheless, there are certain landmark events in Proust's life which cannot be overlooked, not the least of which was his doctor-father's decision to make allowances for his frail son's self-indulgent dependence upon his mother. Before Proust reached the age of ten, it became evident that allergic reactions to common airborne substances posed a serious medical problem. The allergy became so severe that even daylight and fresh air became as toxins to his increasingly asthmatic condition. He was, in fact, to die prematurely at the age of fifty-one of asthma-related complications aggravated by exhaustion, medication, and pneumonia.

It was his physical delicacy, his not working at a regular job as a youth, and his hypochrondriacal ways (aggravated by his parents' deaths in his early manhood) that helped to give him the reputation of dilettantishness. He was also the cultural product of the female-dominated salons and felt like a weakling elder of his father's two sons - thus being regarded by many as effeminate. Proust kept strange hours due to his allergies, frequently going out only in the evening; he was financially secure, having come from a solid bourgeois family; and was given to writing material which many of his acquaintances considered wearisome reading. It was his writing of *Remembrance of Things Past* which allowed him to break away from the stereotype mold of the salon worldling.

PROUST'S MIXED JEWISH-CHRISTIAN HERITAGE

The fact that Marcel Proust was of mixed Jewish and Catholic heritage was monumentally significant to his life and work. There is a nearly perfect blend of the Hebraic and the Roman which gave his work appeal to the Anglo-Saxon Protestant world, and it seems that Proust was likewise attracted to the literature of that world's preeminent country, England. There is, however, another phenomenon in Proust's work which seems inextricably tied to his mixed heritage: the phenomenon in *Remembrance of Things Past* known as "involuntary memory" which involves numerous highly significant and penetrating passages. A sensory experience of the present will be involved in an interplay with a past experience and will suddenly draw us into timeless eternity. It is something we could almost call a symbolic counterpart to transubstantiation - for one series of objects will create a sensation, giving the subject or partaker an almost mystical union with a presence which is the past itself bound into the present. This vision of the seeming past as an actual presence and as eternal reality might have been heightened by his mixed parentage, for it is frequently the case for people of mixed religious background to scrutinize spiritual phenomena with hypersensitive vision rather than to passively accept doctrine. It has been remarked that Proust was not a practicing Catholic as an adult, but he was taken to Mass regularly as a boy and held a life-long fascination for Catholic churches, their altars, flowers, and stained-glass windows. Much of Proust's most beautiful prose is suffused in a religious consciousness, and bears the marks of a keen inner consciousness of transubstantiation in the "precious moment" sequences which include those vastly important ones involving "involuntary memory."

Proust was constantly amid Catholics in Illiers and Paris, and seemed to form a consciousness of certain substances being consecrated and undergoing mystical transformation to bring a sacred presence to the partaker - as is the case with the tea and madeleine which brings a nearly sacred childhood back intact to the narrator of *Remembrance of Things Past*. Proust, the half-Jew living in predominantly Catholic Paris and who was in his own inner exile, reminds us of another 20th-century author of Jewish heritage who lived in another predominantly Christian city. We are reminded of Franz Kafka of Prague who had his own fascination for the Christian doctrine of salvation, but who seemed never to succeed in his desperate exiled attempts to grasp its firsthand experience.

PROUST AND DEITY

The great early biographer of Marcel Proust, Léon Pierre-Quint, suggested that, despite Proust's contact with formal Christianity,

God was not present in Proust's life. Deity, however, may manifest itself in a man's life as an aesthetic life force as well as a purely religious phenomenon in the traditional theological sense. The two may, in fact, mingle and need not be considered as mutually exclusive entities. Proust's evident withdrawal from formal religion in adulthood may well be rooted back to the fact that his beloved mother retained her Jewish faith and the two parents avoided religious discussions. Not only was there an absence of parental spiritual confrontations, but there was a heavy predilection for the scientific in Proust's family as well. Both Proust's father and his younger brother were highly prominent physicians who could very well have been guilty of scientific arrogance, for this seems to be Proust's overriding attitude toward physicians in *Remembrance of Things Past*. Proust's awareness of not just the divine but the celestial in art is surely a contact with God, for it is an ecstasy born out of transcending time and touching eternity. It also resembles nirvana, the most exalted and penetrating of religious experiences of the Eastern mystics. This is the kind of experience that is transposed into an artistic context in *Le Temps retrouvé (The Past Recaptured)* (note the capitalization of "Temps") when the Proustian narrator comes around to his resolve to write his novel while attending the last matinee at the Hôtel de Guermantes. It is this communion with the Absolute which, in fact, becomes the main **theme** of *Remembrance of Things Past* - the nirvana of art - the firsthand intuitive experience of Being - of suspension from time and its ravages, which seems only to come after that conditioning which comes through ordeals of suffering (another main **theme** of the work, embodied in Vinteuil and his music). Proust's art is the isolation and preservation of his ultimate moments of joy on the written page, and then examining and analyzing them as the gem expert would scrutinize the facets, reflections, and colorations of precious stones.

BRIGHT NOTES STUDY GUIDE

CHRONOLOGY OF EVENTS IN THE LIFE AND TIMES OF MARCEL PROUST

1870 Prussians took Alsace.

1871 First year of the Third Republic. The greatness of France threatened with decline.

1871 July 10: Marcel Proust was born in suburban Auteuil of Paris, immediately after the upheaval of the Commune and the German Occupation. His father was Dr. Adrien Proust, a renowned physician and native of Illiers (fictional Combray) in Beauce. His mother was Jeanne Weil (Proust), a Jewess from Alsace-Lorraine. They lived at 9 Boulevard Malesherbes in Paris and were well-to-do financially. Marcel leaned more toward his mother in affection than toward his aloof, business-like father.

1873 Birth of Robert Proust, Marcel's younger brother, who was of a much stronger physical constitution than Marcel and who followed in his father's footsteps to become a prestigious doctor.

1880 Marcel's first recorded attack of asthma. His contact with illness, confinement, and doctors was very influential in the formation of his attitudes and creations. Profuse clinical **imagery** and dislike for physicians is rampantly prevalent in his work. Proust's progressive asthma was incurable, possibly psychosomatic and neurological in origin.

1882-1889 The school years at the Lycée Concdorcet were fulfilling for Proust despite his allergies, for the clerical discipline had moderated with secularization and Proust met many men who were to profoundly influence his life. Among them was Darlu, the master in philosophy. Acquaintances among his precocious school friends included Daniel Halévy and Jacques Bizet (the son of the composer and wife who was to become the influential Mme. Straus whose salon Proust frequented). Proust's studies of the natural sciences at the urging of his father influenced his writing in its profusion of botanical, chemical, and zoological imagery.

1889 Proust received his baccalaureate and spent, oddly enough, a rather fulfilling year in the 76th Infantry Regiment in Orleans, during which time he met Anatole France, who at times harshly criticized Proust and who seems to be the model for Bergotte.

1889 September 25: Charles Kenneth Scott-Moncrieff was born in Sterlingshire, Scotland. Henri Bergson's thesis, "Essai sur les données immédiates de la conscience," appeared.

1890-1896 Period of great social activity and literary beginnings.

1891-1893 Studies at the École des Sciences Politique, at the Law School, and at the Sorbonne where he attended Bergson's lectures and absorbed his ideas on psychological time as distinguished from chronological time. Bergson was in 1891 to marry Mlle. Neuberger, a relative of Proust's mother. Proust's father had hoped that Marcel might become a diplomat or a lawyer, areas in which Proust had little faith. Proust caricatures the hollowness of diplomats in the composite M. de Norpois. Also, during this time, Proust began to frequent the salons of the aristocratic quarter of Paris, the Faubourg Saint-Germain, penetrating it despite his Jewish heritage. He met the composer Reynaldo Hahn whose interest in music influenced Proust and who became his close friend.

1892-1893 First literary essays in the highly successful *Le Banquet*, which Proust founded in Mme. Straus's salon.

1893 Proust's contact with Count Robert de Montesquiou began. Some observers note a similarity between him and the Baron de Charlus.

1893-1896 Articles and stories in *La Revue Blanche*.

1895 Proust travels to Normandy, his model and inspiration for Balbec.

1895-1899 Relatively inactive period marked by deterioration of health. Jean Santeuil written but relegated to the reject pile uncompleted, not to be published until some thirty years after his death. Much of the germ of *À la Recherche du temps perdu (Remembrance of Things Past)* was taking shape in the plot, structure, and characterizations of this "dry run" - but Proust's genius was dormant at this stage. He abandoned Jean Santeuil for the John Ruskin translations.

1896 Les Plaisirs et les Jours, Proust's first published book of stories, poems, and sketches bearing marked influences from Charles Baudelaire and other Symbolistes.

1898 Proust took a consuming interest in the Dreyfus Affair as a pro-Dreyfusard. Many believed that Alfred Dreyfus was prosecuted on circumstantial evidence for allegedly selling French classified military data to Germany. The litigation polarized France at all social levels because the issues of both treason and anti-Semitism were involved. The aristocracy tended to be anti-Dreyfus and the bourgeoisie pro-Dreyfus. Even though Dreyfus was finally judged innocent, the repercussions of the affair are evident in much French literature, including *Remembrance of Things Past*.

1899 Proust began working on translating the English art philosopher, John Ruskin, who influenced Proust in his responsiveness to art and architecture. He inspired Proust's trip to Venice and stimulated his scholarship in Venetian art and art criticism.

1900 Death of John Ruskin. Proust worked on *The Bible of Amiens (La Bible d' Amiens)*. Proust's family moved to 45 rue de Courcelles. Proust traveled to Venice and Padua with his mother, a trip reappearing in *Remembrance of Things Past*.

1902 Proust's health deteriorated further, frequently confining him to his bed.

1903 Death of Proust's father.

1903-1905 Articles published by *Le Figaro*.

1904 Publication of Proust's critical annotated translation of Ruskin's *The Bible of Amiens (La Bible d'Amiens)* by Mercure de France.

1905 Death of Proust's mother.

"On Reading" published in *Renaissance Latine*. Publication of Proust's translation of Ruskin's *Sésame and Lillies, Sésame et les lys*, by Mercure de France. Beginnings of the quasi-critical Centre Sainte Beuve. Transition from Proust-critic to Proust-novelist.

1906 The blow of losing his parents made Proust's allergies worse, which drove him to a hermit's existence at 102 Boulevard Haussmann, where he remained within cork walls and sealed windows until 1919.

1907 Beginnings of *À la Recherche du temps perdu (Remembrance of Things Past)* originally conceived as a three-volume work with the conclusion of *Le Temps retrouvé (The Past Recaptured)* and the "Overture" sequence of *Du Côté de chez Swann (Swann's Way)* being written first.

1908 Proust continued to work on his novel cycle as a virtual hermit, the novel cycle gradually mushrooming from the original three-volume idea to an eventual seven-novel set.

1909 Proust continued on his project, drawing influence on love attitudes by 1910 from reading such English works as Thomas Hardy's *The Well Beloved, Jude the Obscure*, and *A Pair of Blue Eyes*, to which he alludes in *La Prisonnière (The Captive)*.

1912 Alfred Agostinelli (a quasi-model for Albertine) becomes Proust's secretary.

1913 Céleste Albaret (a model for Françoise) becomes Proust's housekeeper. Agreement by Bernard Grasset to publish *Du Côté de chez Swann (Swann's Way)* at Proust's own expense after unsuccessful attempts with other publishers.

1914 Outbreak of World War I. Death of Agostinelli in an airplane accident. Some suggest that this inspired the reference to Albertine's sudden death by a fall from a horse. Proust stayed in Paris during the war, observing tumultuous changes in social attitudes as well as personal acquaintances.

1918 After the war gap in Proust's publishing, *À l'Ombre des jeunes filles en fleurs (Within a Budding Grove)* was published by Gallimard which also published a reissue of *Du Côté de chez*

Swann (Swann's Way). (Nouvelle Revue Francaise [N.R.F.] is part of Gallimard, Paris.)

1919 Publication of *Pastiches et Mélanges* (N.R.F.) much of which had appeared piecemeal in 1908-09. This collection was a critical work containing parodies of the method and style of seventeenth-century writers' portraiture of characters - a group who were among Proust's most important literary predecessors. Proust received Prix Goncourt for *À l'Ombre des jeunes filles en fleurs (Within a Budding Grove)* which made him famous.

Proust moved to 44 rue Hamelin where he lived in cork-sealed seclusion writing *À la Recherche du temps perdu (Remembrance of Things Past)* until his death.

1920 *Le Côté de Guermantes* (I and II) (*The Guermantes Way*) published (N.R.F.). Generally good critical response. *Sodome et Gomorrhe (Cities of the Plain)* (I) published (N.R.F.). Generally poor critical response.

1921 Proust sees Vermeer's "View of Delft."

1922 *Sodome et Gomorrhe* (II) published (N.R.F.), last of his work to be published in his lifetime.

1922 September: First review of C. K. Scott-Moncrieff's English translation, *Remembrance of Things Past*, in *London Times Literary Supplement*. November 18: Proust's death from pneumonia at age 51.

1923 Posthumous publication of *La Prisonnière (The Captive)* (N.R.F.). *Swann's Way* published by Chatto and Windus.

1924 *Within a Budding Grove* published by Chatto and Windus.

1925 *Albertine Disparue (The Sweet Cheat Gone)*, material drawn out of Proust's manuscript La Fugitive, is published (N.R.F.).

The Guermantes Way published by Chatto and Windus.

1927 *Le Temps retrouvé (The Past Recaptured)* published despite fragmentation of narrative and inconsistencies in plot and chronology (N.R.F.).

Cities of the Plain published by Chatto and Windus.

1928 *Chroniques* published by Gallimard.

1929 *The Captive* published by Chatto and Windus.

1930 February 28: Death of C. K. Scott-Moncrieff at age 40 in Rome of complications from illness contracted during active World War I service. He had completed all of *Remembrance of Things Past* except the final novel, *The Past Recaptured*, which has subsequently been translated several times: the most recent version is a thoroughly edited translation by Andreas Mayor. *The Sweet Cheat Gone* published by Chatto and Windus.

1932 *The Past Recaptured* published by Chatto and Windus.

1952 *Jean Santeuil*, Proust's unfinished and abandoned novel, published by Gallimard.

1954 *Contre Sainte-Beuve*, a fictional critique of Sainte-Beuve's analytical method, published by Gallimard. *Nouveaux*

Mélanges published by Gallimard. Complete three-volume annotated set of the entire seven novels of *À la Recherche du temps perdu* published in a thorough critical edition by the Bibliothèque de la Pléiade of Editions Gallimard, Paris. Pierre Clarac and André Ferre, editors.

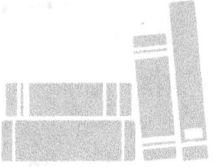

MARCEL PROUST

LITERARY AND PHILOSOPHICAL INFLUENCES

INFLUENCE OF THE FRENCH NEO-CLASSICISTS

One of Marcel Proust's greatest gifts was his mastery of character portrayal, particularly those types of character portrayal influenced by the French Neo-Classical writers of the seventeenth century. These included various oblique forms of character presentation, painstakingly creating characters through seemingly insignificant gestures, through others' reactions to them, or through the subjective reactions of the narrator. Proust's characterizations are not confined solely to Classical devices; many are conceived along Bergsonian lines of flux and illogical change. This latter aspect shall be discussed at length later.

The two primary writers who dealt with personages of the French seventeenth century Neo-Classical Age were the Duc de Saint-Simon (1675-1755) who was Proust's favorite writer of memoirs, and Madame (Marquise) de Sévigné (1626-1696) who was a Parisian epistolary writer. A strong link to Saint-Simon becomes apparent in Proust's portrayal of social stratification and courtly life in *À la Recherche du temps perdu (Remembrance of Things Past)*, to which he refers as "the memoirs of Saint-Simon of another period," Proust's period being the "fin de siècle" and turn into the twentieth century.

Proust's criticism of the aristocracy becomes a basic criticism of "snobisme" - the underlying principle by which the Faubourg Saint-Germain imposed its pattern on all levels of society. It was from Saint-Simon that Proust derived his critique of society; and it was from Sévigné that he drew much of his ready wit and shrewd **satire**. His memorable "pastiche" technique was drawn from both Saint-Simon and de Sévigné although Proust himself was reputedly a phenomenal natural mimic. Through the developed "pastiche" technique, however, he was to draw an intriguing comic vision, utilizing certain characters' idiosyncrasies of appearance, and peculiarities of speech and manner. Numerous of his characters are composites of acquaintances done in "pastiche," among whom some of the more striking are Mme. Verdurin, Dr. Cottard, and Françoise. The prose style of the Classicists is also marked in Proust in his absorption of their leisurely complexities of sentence structure, laden with lengthy successions. The Classical tradition is strong in much French literature, regardless of how modern the work may be: one may observe references to other artists and luminaries of the Renaissance throughout *À la Recherche du temps perdu (Remembrance of Things Past)* in their roles as models. A striking example is the role of Racine's "Phaedra" as a model for perfection in La Berma's dramatic art.

INFLUENCE OF THE ROMANTICS

Proust was not only touched by influence from the seventeenth century but from the succeeding centuries as well. Among the

Romantics influential to Proust were Vicomte François-René de Chateaubriand (1768-1848) who wrote in his best fictional work, Mémoires d'Outre-tombe, of his growth from childhood following his creative life up to 1840. There is something of the childhood reminiscence and of the creative autobiography of Chateaubriand's work in the story of little Marcel's "invisible vocation." Proust's *À la Recherche du temps perdu (Remembrance of Things Past)* was also influenced by the Romantic pre-Symboliste, Gérard Labrunie, known as Gérard de Nerval (1808-1855), in whose work early developments in multiple or split personality may be found. The **theme** of a succession of loves who emerge as incarnations of one being or mental projections of that being appears in his collection, Les Filles de feu (1854) of which the memorable and highly influential "Sylvie" is a part. Chateaubriand, de Nerval, and Baudelaire each receive mention in a critical passage in *Le Temps retrouvé (The Past Recaptured)*.

INFLUENCE OF THE REALISTS AND NATURALISTS

Proust's major gift to literature was his penetration of inner realities and of states of spirit which cannot meet the eye and which defy logic, but his prose technique is not without an inordinate scientific vision and sense of the microscope. A significant part of the French mentality, handed down from the Renaissance and Classicism, is a sense of exactitude of detail, clarity of logic, and "scientisme." The French language even became the international language of diplomacy for its exactitudes in every turn of phrase, not possessing however the sense of mystery and ambiguity of the Germanic languages.

The high-water mark of French **Realism** was reached in the compressed and highly revised, yet painstakingly detailed, style of Gustave Flaubert (1821-1880) whose basically omniscient and impersonal prose narrative was invested with scrupulous word selection in quest of "le mot juste." Flaubert was a contemporary of the heralds of literary positivism and scientisme of which the standard bearers in criticism pertaining to analytical method were Charles-Augustin Sainte-Beuve (1804-1869) and Hippolyte Taine (1828-1893). Proust's style bears characteristics of both "le mot juste" and scientific analysis, particularly in his **imagery**, characterizations, and social comment. It also bears the mark of embryonic internal monologue which was manifesting itself in Flaubert's *Madame Bovary* and in Alain-Fournier's *Le Grand Meaulnes*.

Among the chief influences on Proust were those of the Naturalistic School - writers who subscribed to ideas of scientific determinism along scientifically deducible hereditary and environmental lines. Among the most significant Naturalists were Honoré Balzac (1799-1850) who portrayed vast panoramas of characters whose external actions and characteristics revealed entire personalities, and Émile Zola (1840-1902) who portrayed vast numbers of reappearing characters along the scientific and deterministic lines of their hereditary afflictions and environmental adversities.

Balzac wrote to inordinate lengths in a sometimes humorous style uniquely his own in his social panorama, *La Comédie Humaine*. Even though its content preceded Proust's story material by some fifty years, the Balzac mark is unmistakably on Proust's material with its intertwined entourage of carefully delineated, recurring characters, and its volumes of social commentary relating to the rise of the merciless, aggressive bourgeoisie and its monetary godhead.

More significant than Honoré Balzac in influencing Proust was Émile Zola, whose analytical technique and excruciating sense of the microscope exemplified Naturalism in its most hardened form. Proust was not what we would classify as a Naturalist, but he utilized numerous elements of the Naturalist's clinically oriented literary procedure in, for example, relating the decadence and depravity of the last Guermantes generation. They suffer from the affliction of total decay which seems to run rampant throughout the Faubourg Saint-Germain - something vaguely akin in conception to the illnesses of the Rougon and Macquart families of the voluminous twenty-volume Rougon-Macquart novel-cycle of Zola. Proust's descriptions of illness and death in *Le Côté de Guermantes (The Guermantes Way)* resemble the work of Zola in their technique, and are enhanced further by a profusion of medical and scientific references with which Proust was familiar through his father and brother. Naturalism as an original or stimulating technique, however, had run its course by the end of the nineteenth century. By the turn of the century, the Naturalistic approach was coming to be regarded as very limited and as easily exhaustible -especially with the dawn of new breakthroughs in man's quest of the inner mind in philosophy and psychology. Perhaps the least limited of the Naturalistic writers influential on Proust was the Russian Naturalist who also used such psychological phenomena as precognition, subconscious symbolism, and premonitory dreams. This Russian writer was Fyodor Dostoevski (1821-1881), more influential upon the modern writers of the mid-twentieth century than any of the other Naturalists.

It should be noted that even though Proust utilized much of the prose techniques of the Naturalists, he reacted against the use of hardened "scientisme" at the expense of all else, as was espoused by such narrowly analytical critics as Saint Beuve. Perhaps this was why Proust so loved the works of the English Realists and Naturalists. Among his favorite English novels were George Eliot's (Mary Ann Evans') *Mill on the Floss* and Thomas

Hardy's *A Pair of Blue Eyes* and *Jude the Obscure*. Proust was also attracted to the philosophical art criticism of the English art critic and writer, John Ruskin.

INFLUENCE OF THE SYMBOLISTES

Even though Proust relied frequently on traditional nineteenth-century methods, his *À la Recherche du temps perdu (Remembrance of Things Past)* is anything but a traditional novel. His work is far more advanced than that of the Naturalists, for Proust's work captures the depths of experience, investing it with symbolic designs of exquisite subtle motifs. Like so many artist-quest novels of the twentieth century, Proust's *À la Recherche du temps perdu* exhibits a basic reaction to Naturalistic externalism by developing narrative with only a barely discernible overt plot line. The novel's structure is developed along an internalized plot rather than along externalized episodes, and develops along its recurring themes, symbols, and image motifs. The only significant **episodes** of the work are those in which the spontaneous retrospective visions of involuntary memory bring the sensory reactions of previous experience into focus. There are also numerous other contemplative and reflective sequences of significance, but they defy episodic designation. The flashes of sudden unwilled memory are logically inexplicable retrievals of the seemingly forgotten past of which motifs are scattered throughout the novel cycle. These experiences which are founded in the subconscious may come forward from the slightest interruptions of unguarded moments or reveries.

Proust's consciousness of reality as a synthesis of past and present perception is partly based on Immanuel Kant's German Idealism which had spread the world over, and on the works of the French "Symboliste" poets which included those of Charles

Baudelaire (1821-1867) and Arthur Rimbaud (1854-1891). "Symbolisme," as distinguished from traditional symbolism in allegory and stock metaphors, utilizes a string or cluster of subtle and evocative **metaphors** suggesting states of soul (état d'âme). Paramount to Proust's technique and vision is his use of the language of poetry, essential in catching the elusive flow of intuition. This is part of Proust's reaction to **Realism** and Naturalism: his work uses the language of poetry in evoking the subconscious, a realm far more vast than the scientifically explicable external conscious. Man's true existence lies in his associative mental processes rather than in the logically deducible external incidents of his temporal life. À la Recherche du temps perdu (Remembrance of Things Past) is what some might call a "Symboliste" novel in its use of symbolic development in a uniquely Proustian metaphorical vision.

Perhaps the most important of all literary influences on Proust is that of Charles Baudelaire, whose concept of "correspondences" involves synaesthesia - a significant modern poetic vision of transferred stimuli and responses between different senses, suggesting an interchangeability of sense perceptions. One familiar with Symboliste poetry can well recall the following lines from Charles Baudelaire's **sonnet** "Correspondences" from the large set of poems, Les Fleurs du Mal (The Flowers of Evil):

Les perfums, les coleurs et le sons répondent,

> **Il est des perfums frais comme des chairs d'enfants,**
>
> **Doux comme les hautbois, verts comme les prairies...**

Poetry defies translation, but one usually is more successful if one attempts to preserve feeling at the possible expense of literal verbal accuracy and impeccable **prosody**. In translating "Correspondences," the cognate title may be preserved, but a somewhat softer English olfactory word than "perfume" would serve this elusive poem better. The following would suffice as an attempt at translation: "Fragrances, colors and sounds are calling back to us, It is the fresh fragrance of baby skin, Sweet as woodwinds, green as meadows..."

Baudelaire's collection *Les Fleurs du Mal* deals with the poet's aspiration to the "ideal" in art and love to overcome the predicament of "spleen" - a state similar to the isolation and depression preceding Marcel's involuntary memory sequences or those involving contemplative revelations similar to involuntary memory. "Correspondences" suggests that visible phenomena possess, in hidden essences, a reality higher than what meets the eye.

As well as being deeply marked by the influence of Charles Baudelaire, Proust's novel is also marked by influence from Arthur Rimbaud (1854-1891), the French poet said to have set the tone of the Symboliste movement in the remarkable childhood work, "Le Bateau Ivre." Among Rimbaud's most radically modern work is the heavily synaesthetic **sonnet** "Voyelles," which suggests correspondences between the various vowel sounds and a musical scale of color. This poem, like so much of Rimbaud's work, is strikingly reminiscent of childhood; and one can readily observe its influence upon Marcel's reflections of sound colorations in place names, noting particularly the section "Place Names: The Name" in *Du Côté de chez Swann (Swann's Way)*. The **theme** of childhood is penetrating in Rimbaud's poems of which a large number of the best were written between the ages of ten and twenty. They appear under the title "Illuminations," which was given to his work when the poet Paul Verlaine had the material published. The objective of the Symbolistes was to capture and impart transcendent, non-verbal sensations in terms of the state of spirit or "state of soul," the "état d'ame." This was, likewise, the objective of Marcel Proust in his conception and treatment of "correspondence"-related, synaesthetic symbolic transfigurations whereby a stimulus upon one sense faculty will evoke a response in another. Some of Proust's most beautiful prose of this sort may be found in the recounting of Mme. de Saint-Euverte's musicale in "Un Amourde Swann" in the first novel.

INFLUENCE OF HENRI BERGSON

Among the philosophical influences on Proust, brief mention has already been made of Immanuel Kant's concept of reality as a synthesis of subjective intuition, but of more immediate philosophical influence than Kant was the influence of Henri Bergson (1859-1941). Bergsonism touches nearly all of the major **themes** plus the basis for conception of *À la Recherche du temps perdu (Remembrance of Things Past)* - the proposition that time is a tensile, elastic substance of which the duration and even the existence is determined by subjective, intuitive processes. Bergson posited access to the dynamic reality of his "vital" philosophy as coming through intuition, which is distinct from static intellect.

While at the Sorbonne, Proust came to know Henri Bergson and became personally, as well as philosophically, close to him. Each reacted against the rigid categories and analytical determinism of nineteenth-century thinkers. Proust became familiar with Bergson's thesis, "Les Données Immediates de la conscience," which had appeared in 1889, just prior to their acquaintance. The underlying foundation of Bergson's thought lay in the dynamic principle of the "elan vital, "whereby nothing takes a fixed or objectively measured state. Bergson touches all of the basic Proustian **themes** in his philosophy: the flow of time; the perpetual flux and mutation of personality; the intuitive recapturing of the unconscious; involuntary, associative memory and the recovery of life through the reality of art.

Bergson's philosophy of time has its basis in "durée mobile" ("mobile duration") - that essential idea that time is not a static, mechanically chronological phenomenon. Rather, time is measured psychologically, having its basis in the subjective point of view of our own individual consciousness. Time may, in fact, be accentuated, halted, or even reversed in our inner minds - the home of real or authentic experience. Memory also plays along non-chronological lines.

Proust's portrayal of characters who almost invariably lack any psychological base of permanence also relates to the Bergsonian idea of the absence of fixedness in life, love, and friendship. A person whom we think we have come to know may change for no logical reason, suddenly and without warning. We may even discover hidden lives that we never thought possible in people we thought we knew. Personality is imbued with flux, and we are all the captives of time.

The role of the unconscious is of great magnitude in Proust whether its evocations come from reverie, in waking from sleep, contemplation of an object, artistic meditation, or involuntary memory. Paramount in evocations of the unconscious is the role of the mental process of intuition, wherein essence and reality reside. This also relates to Kantian thought, as has been mentioned, for Proust's turning of his mind's eye inward in search of a principle of unity within himself is derived from Kantian idealism. It is the sense of this inner reality that made Proust skeptical of the scientific idea that truth lay in external reality and that it can only be apprehended by the intelligence. Proust's vision is one whereby reality is apprehended and captured by intuition, then set down and minutely examined by intelligence. The Bergson-influenced roles of involuntary memory and recovery of life through the artistic vision of **metaphor** shall be treated in the separate sections which follow.

MARCEL PROUST

INVOLUNTARY MEMORY

Comment has already been made upon the process of involuntary memory as it could be possibly related to Proust's religious background. At this point, however, one could also relate involuntary memory to Bergsonism, for it is inextricably intertwined with the concept of psychological time as opposed to chronological time. It is an integral part of the Proustian creative process, for it is contingent upon the fact that true reality lies within and that our subconscious minds contain memories and ideas which our conscious minds believe that we have forgotten. This process of seeming forgetting is sometimes referred to by critics as "oubli," the French word for "oblivion."

These vital realities which reside beneath the surface in the vast subconscious are evoked usually by seemingly commonplace things that our conscious intelligence would overlook so far as importance of any magnitude is concerned. Seemingly trivial sensations experienced in early childhood may burrow so deeply into our subconscious minds that we may consider them forgotten; then, at some unguarded moment during a period of boredom or decreased mental activity, they may be evoked suddenly by analogous sensations. In this process, we actually become the selves that we once were at some previous time, as we come to experience firsthand once again our childhood or youth. Distant yesterdays become one and the same with today, and we become mystically suspended from the apparently relentless march of time: we are resurrected to touch eternity in what becomes a fourth dimension.

There are numerous examples in *À la Recherche du temps perdu (Remembrance of Things Past)* of this firsthand retrieval of the seemingly lost past as well as examples of its almost taking place. We could refer to the latter as incipient involuntary memory, where something precious and elusive is signaled but does not quite solidify. Even though memory does not crystallize from the incipient experience, there does emerge a feeling of "deja vu," or a heightened sense of reality bordering on memory. Sometimes, these moments will take us into presentiments of the future rather than memories of the past - giving us a play of anticipation or premonition rather than a retrospective one of recollection.

With only a few exceptions, these moments of heightened awareness are moments of rare joy and exhilaration, coming frequently and catching us unaware at times of depression. Chance associations of objects and sensations bring us to relive experience which at once reaches new heights: it is now no longer commonplace and easily forgotten as it was in the original past. For brief moments, memory becomes an integral part of the creative process, and the artist-type who recognizes certain enlivened experiences as extraordinary will then hurry to preserve them on paper or canvas before they disappear again as rapidly as they came. The retrieved past holds more than the past itself, for we are in the midst of an oscillation and simultaneous unification of the two, as well as an interplay with the future. The yield is an eternal bonding of all time - past, present, and future - into an absolute unity akin to the nirvana of Eastern mysticism, whereby all of our trivial worldly obsessions are extinguished with our ego as we are brought to experience salvation. In Bergsonian terms, we are simultaneously in different points in the flux of nonchronological time, and come to experience something like a space-time fourth dimension. Mystically, we experience firsthand the transcendence of Being, entering into a timelessness with the eternal All, the prime cause or beginning of things.

Bergsonism relates also to art, for it is the rare property of true art that seizes hold of and preserves the fleeting, precious moments of heightened consciousness. In Proust, the instrument by which this is accomplished is "metaphor." In the quest for unlocking hidden essences, the goal may be achieved by a meditative liberation from the exigencies of time, through contemplative reverie, or through involuntary memory. Contemplating great works of art as well as one's own creative inspiration will have the effect of meditation - as in the case of Marcel's viewing Elstir's seascapes, reading Bergotte's novels, or observing Bergotte's spellbound reaction to Vermeer's "View of Delft."

The actual sequences in *À la Recherche du temps perdu (Remembrance of Things Past)* which involve the above-mentioned time deliverances will be discussed individually as they relate to the narrator Marcel, to Bergsonism, and to the Proustian artistic vision as each of the separate novels of the cycle is examined.

MARCEL PROUST

PROUST'S CONCEPTION OF METAPHOR

Closely associated with Marcel Proust's vision of inner reality, of involuntary memory, and other variants of time deliverance is his unique technique and vision, "metaphor." This bears a close kinship, also, to the Baudelarean conception of "correspondences" wherein the Symboliste's idea of reality lies in the mystical or psychic relationship between subject and object. Proust's "**metaphor**" also carries overtones of Kantianism and Bergsonism: there is a correlation of the Kantian synthesis of subjective reflections as reality and the Bergsonian predilection with the effect of time interactions upon the subject. Proust's "metaphor," unlike such attempts by other contemporary and more recent authors, carries an evocative power and intensity that can be attributed to the strength and beauty of his **imagery**. There is a perfect balance between the influence of philosophy and the striking originality of unsurpassed literary creation. Proust's unrivaled **imagery** is the medium through which disparate sights, sounds, tastes, and smells may coalesce in perfect, frequently synaesthetic relationships.

   Metaphor, however, constitutes more than mere elaborate figurative language in Proustian literature: it is the embodiment of a full artistic vision of perception. It is, in fact, articulated in several outstanding passages of *À la Recherche du temps perdu*. A memorable example of this sort of passage on artistic creation of which the underpinnings are based on "**metaphor**" appears in *A l'Ombre de jeunes filles en fleurs (Within a Budding Grove)* as Marcel examines some of Elstir's seascapes in his Balbec studio and, at the same time, experiences a sense of liberation and firsthand revelation. Another outstanding example of this sort of material appears in *La Prisonnière (The Captive)* when the artistically matured writer Bergotte suddenly experiences firsthand a mystical union with Jan Vermeer's color-metaphor of the spellbinding little patch of yellow wall in the "View of Delft." It is in that one spot on the canvas that Vermeer has been able to capture and subdue the transience of worldly existence, bringing to his work a contact with the absolute harmony and peace of eternity. It is only in dying that Bergotte apprehends the transcendence of something so seemingly commonplace as a cast of sunlight on a tiny portion of wall. Interestingly enough, there is no pure excursus on **metaphor** itself in *Du Côté de chez Swann (Swann's Way)* but Proust's own art reaches its greatest sustained purity and vision in this the most finely wrought novel from an artistic standpoint. It is in this work that we are introduced to the prominent artist figures, and suggestions are made to forecast their immanent artistic ascendency. Some of Proust's most beautiful and memorable synaesthetic metaphorical prose on art appears in the recounting of Mme. de Saint-Euverte's musicale in "Un Amour de Swann." There is an almost unbearable beauty and magic in the rich, metaphorically conceived sections of *Du Côté de chez Swann (Swann's Way)*, "Combray" and "Place Names: the Name" in their **imagery** and motif structure. The final **exposition** on "**metaphor**" gives a recapitulative route to artistic truth at the novel cycle's end, appearing in the musicale sequence of *Le Temps retrouvé (The Past Recaptured)*. An extended section on Proust's style and on the novel cycle as an artistic unity will appear following examination of the individual novels.

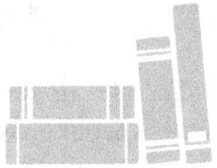

REMEMBRANCE OF THINGS PAST

BASIC STRUCTURE

PROUST'S FRENCH TITLE: À LA RECHERCHE DU TEMPS PERDU

Marcel Proust derived his title in part from that of a novel by Honoré Balzac, *Les Illusions Perdues,* and in part from an old provincial saying that suggests that time lost can never again be recovered ("Temps perdu ne se retrouvé point"). Comment shall be made upon the English title, *Remembrance of Things Past,* in a section concerned with the translation in general.

GENERAL NOTE ON THE STRUCTURE OF THE WORK AS A WHOLE

Chronologically, this "roman fleuve," or "river novel," covers a vast forty-year span extending from before the "fin de siècle" to the conclusion of World War I. Originally Proust had the work blueprinted as a three-volume work with *Du Côté de chez Swann (Swann's Way)* focusing on the bourgeoisie, *Le Côté de Guermantes (The Guermantes Way)* focusing on the aristocracy, and *Le Temps retrouvé (The Past Recaptured)* focusing on the redemptive value of recaptured psychological time. The novel cycle grew from its original conception as a three-volume work to a monumental seven-novel work built in tiers of which *Du Côté' de chez Swann* is the base.

The overriding **theme** of the cycle is time and, structurally, it goes full circle from the first word, "Longtemps...." to the final word, "temps," recounting a young man's growth and his quest to become a writer. The quest of the entire *À la Recherche du temps perdu* is for artistic salvation, and it follows the triadic pattern of life, death, and resurrection. The novel begins at a point in an almost indeterminate present, carries us back and forward through Swann's and Marcel's lives, and eventually leaves us again in the present.

Not only does the novel cycle develop itself in terms of size and around time's aesthetic and eternal aspects, but it also finds sustained structural elements in its character portrayals and imagery.

Basic to the novel's development and unification through characters, for instance, is the role of Charles Swann as an inter-class and inter-character linking element. Not only are nearly all the other characters in the cycle in some way linked to Swann socially, but the narrator Marcel's loves and disillusionments form psychological parallels to Swann's early love affair with Odette de Crecy. As the huge "roman fleuve" rolls onward, Marcel and the reader come to realize that all love seems to follow the Swann pattern. All of the great love relationships of the work are unfulfilled: Swann's for Odette, Marcel's for Gilberte and Albertine, Robert de Saint Loups' for Rachel, and the Baron de Charlus' for Morel. Of all the loves recounted in the work, the filial love of Marcel for his mother and his grandmother seems to be the purest, though that too is tinged with a basic sadness and is not immune to loss. The Proustian love relationship, of which the basic pattern is set in Swann's, follows from idealizing the love object, through a falling away through love, to the **catastrophes** of jealousy and ultimate loss.

Another basic structural element relating to the characters sustained throughout the cycle is the recurrence of psychological and sociological flux in their sense of impermanence and mutation. The majority of the characters, especially those of the crumbling Guermantes circle, have no permanent psychological base. They live as hypocritical weathervanes, seeking the transitory pleasures of the given moment in prestigious friendships, political security, and social status. Some are so transparently superficial that frequently the character we feel assured we know in one section of the work will emerge afterward as quite a different person. Detail will be presented in sections on the characters as each novel is studied. Many of the titled nobility, as well as their common counterparts, have secret lives and vices that we know not of until we quite unexpectedly see them at unguarded moments, or when a clue is otherwise inadvertently dropped by either an acquaintance or by general rumor. Examples of characters whose inner selves are in such manner revealed include Odette de Crecy, Bloch, Robert de Saint Loup, Albertine, and the notorious Baron de Charlus. Likewise, great gifts and talents may surface surprisingly and unexpectedly in characters like Dr. Cottard, Master Biche, La Berma, Bergotte, and M. Vinteuil.

The sense of flux, impermanence, and change in *À la Recherche du temps perdu (Remembrance of Things Past)* is not limited to just certain clusters of characters, such as those of the Guermantes circle, but manifests itself in the novel cycle's overall form as well. Socially, the final stroke in the Proustian process of flux is the ultimate destratification and leveling off of the class structure ("déclassement"), but overtones of flux may be noted in the seeming mercurial looseness of the work as a whole as well. Ultimately, however, this voluminous "river novel" locks itself into a nearly perfect construct of permanence amid change in *Le Temps retrouvé (The Past Recaptured)*. The final moment of involuntary memory in the Guermantes' library at the end locks the others very well into their own places in a huge kaleidoscopic design. The final sentence in the last novel also has a combined effect with the first in the entire work, of setting the whole *À la Recherche du temps perdu* into a fluid and yet fixed circular form. As in any great poetry, the form of the work should bear manifestations of the content and, ideally, should become one with it. In this case, the novel cycle's form is imbued finally with the sense of permanence and indestructibility as Marcel's final artistic revelation and resolve to write his novel.

At certain points, *À la Recherche du temps perdu* appears to have been put together in almost random fashion, growing seemingly without design from a three-novel work to a seven-novel work, and resembling at times a succession of unconnected memoirs and pastiches à la Saint-Simon and de Sévigné. Admittedly, toward the end, the ordering of certain events seems jumbled, and chronological disorientation of Swann's third-person narrative in the midst of Marcel's first-person narration is sometimes puzzling. We seem to literally ramble from Marcel's childhood into a story predating the narrator's birth. We pass through more childhood memories in the second novel and enter into his love for Gilberte Swann and his early acquaintance with Albertine Simonet whom he first encounters from a distance amid a little band ("jeunes filles en fleurs") on a Balbec vacation. In the third novel of the cycle, we seem to fall into more coincidences, of which there is a profusion in the plot, and follow Marcel through his infatuation for the Duchesse de Guermantes. In the fourth and fifth novels, we encounter the abysmal depravity of a fallen and impotent aristocracy, and Marcel falls in love with Albertine. The fifth novel is loosely drawn around Marcel's jealousy for Albertine both when she is living and posthumously, and continues through the sixth and seventh novels. The final novel brings us to the changes brought on by World War I, but more importantly, it presents Proust's sophisticated theory of art in expository form. It is this **theme** of the redemptive power of art and the final expository recapitulation which give full artistic unity to an otherwise loosely constructed story. The role of sustained images and synaesthesia in the construct of the work as an artistic unity will be discussed later in a full section. Artistically, however, we progress in *À la Recherche du temps perdu (Remembrance of Things Past)* from firsthand sensations which bring artistic identity and expanded awareness to the narrator to the theoretical analyses in later volumes. The enormous cycle of literature seems to be charted with extreme care in its gradual and consistent evolution from recounting of experience to recounting of theory. Some later writers have followed a pattern resembling Proust's but have chosen to relate the theory underlying a previously written novel in an altogether separate theoretical treatise. Albert Camus was to do this twice: first in his theorizing of material in L'Étranger in *Le Mythe de Sysiphe*, and again in his theorizing of La Peste in *L'Homme révolté*. Proust, however, possessed the consummate genius which enabled him to artistically mingle analysis on a sophisticated level with spontaneous first-person narration.

Finally, in synopsizing the basic structure of *À la Recherche du temps perdu* before examining each novel individually, one may examine the role of certain patterns in recurrent **imagery** and motifs in the work. Images emerge as motifs in recurrence, and they ultimately crystallize into clusters of symbols as they become identified with the cycle's main **themes** of society, love, death, time, memory, and art. Because the visual faculty is the one which most readily captures those sensations that are logically irreducible, much Proustian **imagery** relates to such illusions of optical perception as light, color, and shadow. **Imagery** surrounding the various sorts of tubes, glasses, and lenses through which a clinician perceives detail is also profuse in Proustian literature, due largely to the laboratory atmosphere of his doctor-father's home, and to his inheritance of that sense of the clinic and the microscope from his literary forebears, the Naturalists.

The predilection for the organic in Proust's **imagery** extends to his gifted use of floral, marine, and zoological images as well. And even though there may have been attempts to keep images sealed intact as in a controlled laboratory environment, Proust's own brilliance of imagination brings his images into their own as they grow and flourish in a vast and magnificent botanical garden. This was no doubt enhanced by the claustrophobic confinement imposed upon the writer by his lethal allergies to the very elements of air and vegetation about which he wrote so profusely. As may well have been the case in religious phenomena, Proust also seemed to observe what lay beyond the commonplace and generally taken for-granted in the botanical, ornithological, aquatic, and zoological. He apprehended, in strange vibrations and pulsations, both the magical and sinister elements of life.

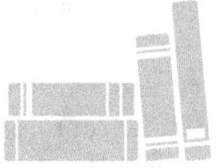

REMEMBRANCE OF THINGS PAST

SIGNIFICANT PLACES

There are places of particular significance in *À la Recherche du temps perdu (Remembrance of Things Past)* which would bear mentioning prior to embarking upon separate studies of the individual novels.

Balbec: the name of this Norman seaside resort area holds a fascination akin to magic for Marcel as a boy whose idealized vision has not yet been tainted by seeing the Balbec of reality. Marcel is taken there by his grandmother and later by his mother and comes to identify Balbec with a smallgauge 1:22 train, with Albertine of a little band of young girls, and with the magnificent Elstir. Its being a resort area is significant, for it allows the author to convincingly mix aristocrats with bourgeoisie and thus launch his major **theme** of "déclassement" as autumn approaches at the conclusion of *A l'Ombre de jeunes filles en fleurs (Within a Budding Grove)*.

Combray: the village where Marcel and his family visited at Aunt Léonie's and which is associated with the unsullied innocence of childhood throughout Marcel's narrative. It is connected with Eastertide, the tea and madeleine, and the redemptive quality of eternal youth.

Doncières: the barracks town, at which Robert de Saint Loup is stationed as a soldier, located on the railway line between Paris and Balbec.

The Faubourg Saint-Germain: the highly stratified stronghold of the aristocracy in Paris, an exclusive quarter in a way resembling the Louisburg Square quarter of old Boston. World War I marks the terminal crumbling away of these old aristocratic quarters as times, mores, and social priorities change.

The Guermantes Way: the pathway leading from Aunt Léonie's mansion toward the Guermantes compound of Combray.

Martinville: a village near Combray where Marcel views the apparent movement of the twin steeples of Martinville and a third one of Vieuxvicq.

The Méséglise Way: the pathway leading from Aunt Léonie's mansion in the direction of Swann's Tansonville.

Montjouvain: a village near Combray at which the Vinteuils lived, which serves structurally to anticipate the events of *Sodome et Gomorrhe (Cities of the Plain)*.

La Raspelière: an exclusive section of the Balbec area, at which the grossly wealthy Verdurins have rented out a country seat from Mme. de Cambremer. Marcel frequently is to take Albertine to dinner at the fashionable restaurant there, during his second visit.

Tansonville: Swann's hawthorn-enclosed estate to which the Méséglise Way leads.

REMEMBRANCE OF THINGS PAST

THE SEVEN NOVELS OF REMEMBRANCE OF THINGS PAST

At certain points in the following study of Proust's novel cycle, references to page numbers will be made regarding highlight passages containing involuntary memory, references to art and **metaphor**, and memorable sustained **imagery**. Those to the English will refer to the Vintage paperback editions of the C. K. Scott-Moncrieff *Remembrance of Things Past*, and those to the French will refer to the three-volume Bibliothèque de la Pléiade edition of *À la Recherche du temps perdu*.

When actual quotation is made, however, the English translation

shall be an original translation by this commentator, following

the Proustian French passage.

These references will appear together in the section on **imagery** and synaesthesia in the study of the metaphorical aspects of Proust's style following the individual examinations of the seven separate novels.

DU CÔTÉ DE CHEZ SWANN (SWANN'S WAY): PUBLISHING HISTORY AND GENERAL INTRODUCTION

The first novel of Proust's cycle was published by Bernard Grasset in 1913 at the author's own expense following unsuccessful attempts with other publishers. Criticism directed at the work included comment upon the overly prolix quality of Marcel's waking reverie at the beginning of the book. Some considered the work dilettantish, of overly ornate style, and of excessive length. Frequently, however, it takes time for a masterpiece to gain appreciation, and it was not until *À l'Ombre des jeunes filles en fleurs (Within a Budding Grove)* received the Goncourt Prize in 1919 that *Du Côté de chez Swann (Swann's Way)* received acclaim, being subsequently reissued by Gallimard.

Today, *Du Côté de chez Swann* is considered to be a twentieth-century masterpiece of rare depths and beauty, and is considered by most critics to be artistically superior to the other six novels of the cycle. It contains far more **imagery** than any one of the other novels, lacks the arduous prolongation of social events, has a sense of the comic, and is devoid of the treatise-like expository passages which bear down upon the work by the fourth novel. If one wished to trace the Proustian evolution of *Du Côté de chez Swann*, one could find part of its genesis in the abandoned Jean Santeuil, which was not published until 1952.

BRIGHT NOTES STUDY GUIDE

PLOT SUMMARY OF DU CÔTÉ DE CHEZ SWANN (SWANN'S WAY)*

Part I: "Overture": Marcel turns about in bed recalling bedrooms of his past, contemplating his magic lantern. He recalls childhood visits to the sheltered and cultivated Combray home of Aunt Léonie amidst elder relatives. Charles Swann visited Marcel's family faithfully, one particularly significant visit leaving its impression on Marcel throughout the work. Marcel was sent to bed early that night without his mother's goodnight kiss because she was busy entertaining Swann. For hours Marcel anxiously awaited Swann's departure. Marcel finally approached his mother, and being still upset after Swann's leaving, she consents to stay beside him overnight. Years later, his mother serves him tea and madeleine, which along with elusive flavors, give an onrush of involuntary memory enabling Marcel to relive his happy Combray childhood.

Part II: "Combray": Marcel recalls childhood, family and neighbors. He aspires to become a writer and writes of passing three steeples. Marcel's people take walks along the Méséglise Way and the Guermantes Way. Captivated by the unattainable, he remembers seeing the young Duchesse de Guermantes in the Combray church and catching his first glimpse of Gilberte.

Part III: "Un Amour de Swann": This is Swann's love story involving Odette, predating Marcel's birth by thirty years, but influential to Marcel's life and parallel to his jealousy-ridden loves for Gilberte and Albertine. Odette introduces Swann to the Verdurins and consorts with de Forcheville.

---

* Permission for plot summaries and quotations has been granted by Random House, Inc., and Alfred A. Knopf, Inc.

Years after, Marcel remembers in the present of playing with Gilberte in the Champs-Élysées, sadly revisiting lost time - seeing that times have changed - realizing that all seems eventually devoured by time.

MAJOR STRUCTURAL AND THEMATIC ELEMENTS OF DU CÔTÉ DE CHEZ SWANN (SWANN'S WAY)

Du Côté de chez Swann is loosely structured in sonata form with the story of Charles Swann's love and jealousy for Odette de Crecy ("Un Amour de Swann") preceded and followed by extended and chronologically disoriented reminiscences by the first-person narrator Marcel.

Despite certain variations or embroidery with sub-themes, most of the thematology and symbolism introduced in *Du Côté de chez Swann* is sustained throughout the seven novels, giving the colossal work symmetry and artistic unity despite digressions, vast length and breadth, and intricate mutating characterizations.

Among the most important **themes** of the novel, which will be elaborated upon separately, are those of childhood and idealization (Combray); snobism and anachronistic stratified society (the two "ways," the "memoirs of Saint-Simon of another period"); love, jealousy, disillusionment (Odette, Gilberte, the Duchesse de Guermantes); music (Vinteuil's "little phrase"); art (the magic lantern, stained glass windows, Swann's vision of personages in terms of famous works of art, Swann's proposed monograph on Vermeer); time, memory, resurrection (tea-madeleine invested with time deliverance, Eastertide); Marcel's "invisible vocation" of writing (passage on the three steeples of Martinville and Vieuxvicq, reference to Bergotte, Marcel's image-laden reflections on the names of such places as Balbec); social events (the two dinners with Mme. Verdurin's "clan," and the fascinating musicale at Mme. de Saint-Euverte's); and disillusionment (Montjouvain, Balbec).

Marcel's Childhood at Combray: The elusive and irretrievable spirit of childhood with its idealizing of unknown realities has captivated numerous writers including the Symboliste poet Arthur Rimbaud whose spontaneous and reflective *Illuminations* could well have influenced Proust's "Place Names: the Name" and the Combray flashback-triggering by his mother's seemingly insignificant tea and madeleine. The magical little village of Combray embodies the idealized, unspoiled vision of pure, innocent childhood. It also captures the essence of provincial French life as it had been lived for hundreds of years, with its tableaus of peasants, flowers, churches, and chateaux. It is at Combray where the narrator Marcel suffused himself in elevated reading and absorbed the leisure-class cultivation of his parents, grandparents, aunts, and uncles. Their circle of Combray friends includes Charles Swann, an art connoisseur, plus the actual artist figures who include M. Vinteuil. Combray is a child's paradise and at its extremities are two worlds forbidden to the genteel middle class-the world of Tansonville and the world of the Guermantes. One of the saddest **themes** of Proust is the gradual and irrevocable fading away of those things associated with the idyllic, insular world of Combray. The "Combray" sequence, however, contains some of Marcel Proust's best prose, of which the descriptions of hawthorns and of the church of St. Hilaire are particularly memorable.

"Snobisme" and Stratified Society: The basic fabric of the social structure in Proust's France comprised the remnants of nineteenth-century life, with its sharp distinctions between various levels of nobility, mutual exclusivity between aristocracy and bourgeoisie, and nearly total exclusion of Jews. *À la Recherche du temps perdu (Remembrance of Things Past)*, however, depicts a gradual process of "déclassement," or destratification, which is barely perceptible in *Du Côté de chez Swann (Swann's Way)* but becomes as an earthquake in subsequent novels. The whole underlying core of this stratification lies in "snobisme," involving a caste-like social identity and arrogance that is almost as rigid amongst the bourgeoisie as it is amongst the descendants of medieval lords. The new professional classes of the Industrial Revolution were just as apt to call the aristocrats "idlers" or "bores" in their own bourgeois salons like Mme. Verdurin's as the aristocrats were apt to exclude what they considered to be vulgar nouveaux riches in the exclusive salons of the Faubourg Saint-Germain.

"Snobisme" runs rampant in the novel cycle and is exposed incisively, often humorously, as Swann the Jew infiltrates salons of not only the gentile bourgeoisie but also of the highest echelons of royalty. Interestingly, too, Swann emerges as a superior human being for his lack of bitter snobbery and his refusal to ridicule and backbite one group to another - a quality which infuriates the hypocritical Mme. Verdurin.

In *Du Côté de chez Swann (Swann's Way)* we have a subtle transition into what will emerge in sharp focus in the following novel in the world of the Norman seacoast resort of Balbec. As in the Verdurin "clan" scenes of the first novel, there is to be a comic vision of "déclassement" as inter-class mingling sets in on an autumnal Balbec. As a document, or as "memoirs of Saint-Simon of another period," Proust's commentary on "snobisme" takes on its darker tones when the **theme** of Dreyfusism is brought into the third novel. In Combray, however, the major underpinning of the novel cycle's structure exists in the two ways which depart from opposite gateways of Aunt Léonie's estate - one way leading through the plain toward Tansonville, and the other leading through the countryside of the Vivonne River toward the Guermantes compound. Through social **conventions** founded on taboo and snobbery, both limits of the two ways are forbidden territory to Marcel, the former through Swann's marriage to his mistress and the latter through caste boundaries excluding the middle class from the Guermantes circle. The "Méséglise" or "Swann's" Way is symbolically the pathway of love and passion; the Guermantes Way is the pathway of society extending upward to its pinnacle, the Faubourg Saint-Germain.

Love, Jealousy, Disillusionment: The basic essence of Proustian love is that it is not focused on a real person, but on an unattainably idealized vision of the lover's imagination. As the beloved becomes more familiar and ordinary, or shows some heretofore unfathomed hidden trait, the lover becomes disillusioned. Nevertheless, if the beloved remains for a while mysterious and enigmatic, the secrets of individualized personality and identity remain uncovered and the person is still endowed with a sense of unattainability. The lure of unattainability brings with it the onslaught of jealousy to the beholder, but in Proustian loves this is ephemeral and ultimately separation occurs. The separation may come by death, or it may come from a relationship's having run its arduous course. Inherent in this course is a Proustian phenomenon known as "intermittence of heart" - strange fluctuations of heat and cooling, oscillations which eventually weaken and fade away, taking with them the memories of passion and jealousy. In *Du Côté de chez Swann (Swann's Way)* the allurement to the unattainable is manifest in Marcel's attraction to the young Duchesse whom he sees in an awesomely beautiful vision in the Combray church of St. Hilaire. This magnificent boyhood moment, coupled with another in a theatre during his adolescence in *Le Côté de Guermantes (The*

Guermantes Way) is offset when she comes to no longer smile to Marcel and his discovery that she is as shrewd and calculating as an ordinary cold woman. Friendships and loves bear that same Bergsonian pattern of flux and impermanence, and the primary significance thematically of *Du Côté de chez Swann (Swann's Way)* is that it sets the Swann - Odette pattern which will be sustained throughout the work in the loves of Marcel-Gilberte, Marcel-Albertine, Saint Loup-Rachel, Saint Loup-Gilberte, and de Charlus-Morel.

Marcel Proust's Use of Music as a Structural Element: Proust had a unique fascination for music and the role which it plays in *À la Recherche du temps perdu (Remembrance of Things Past)* is all-encompassing for it involves all of the other main **themes** of the work as well - love, time, disillusionment, jealousy, resurrection through art, immortality. Specifically, the Vinteuil "little phrase," which first appears in a sonata in the Swann circuit and later appears in a septet in the Marcel circuit, touches all the important **themes** and frequently recurs with subtle artistry throughout the cycle. It is perhaps the most significant of the structural unifying elements, for it not only underscores major plot elements but also begets long, interrelated lineages of fabulous synaesthetic **imagery**. The "little phrase" lilts about Mme. Verdurin's salon and plays upon Swann's ears and mind before he is even familiar with the work to which it belongs. It subsequently emerges as the **theme** song, or anthem, of Swann's tormented pursuit and love for Odette. Swann is eventually to hear Vinteuil's elusive strains again and to discover what they are, learning not only their musical identity, but their place in punctuating the various phases of his love affair as well. The musical composition serves as a leitmotif in linking the common points of Swann's and Marcel's love relationships, thus serving as an inter-plot unifying element. Its significance at the evening musicale of Mme. de Saint-Euverte is paramount, for it is at this gathering that the musical phrase signals the end of Swann's consuming love for Odette, and even though he marries her afterward it is only for pragmatic reasons.

Art: The **theme** of great art is preeminent in *À la Recherche du temps perdu (Remembrance of Things Past)* for it is through art that the exigencies and consequent ravages of time are conquered. True art brings about a mystical union whereby the past, present, and future become all one - eternal permanent Being. True artistic inspiration approaches nirvana, for all the trivialities of ego are extinguished and the true Self is projected in either artistic creation or the thorough-going experience of another's art which inherently involves one's own capacity for creation. The whole **theme** of art in Proust is contingent upon the kind of metaphorical relationship which exists in correspondences between subject and object - the purity of which determines the degree of suspension from time and flight into eternity. In *Du Côté de chez Swann (Swann's Way)* we have superlative prose suggesting this deliverance from ordinary time-bound existence to a kind of timeless super-presence of the past in the present.

Marcel's first contact with art comes in his contemplation of the colors and legends of the magic lantern which suffuse his unfamiliar Balbec hôtel room as he himself hovers in a sleepless reverie. The magic lantern becomes a sustained Proustian motif which blends into other motifs such as the stained-glass windows whose depictions of legendary and historical France fascinate Marcel. It is also in *Du Côté de chez Swann* that we become aware of Charles Swann's intended manuscript on Johann (Jan) Vermeer, of Marcel's upcoming acquaintance with Bergotte through a book lent by Bloch, of his upcoming contemplation of Elstir's works, and his first acquaintance with the name La Berma.

Marcel's "Invisible Vocation": Interrelated with art and contemplation, the **theme** of Marcel's literary career becomes one of the master themes, if not the main story, of the entire *À la Recherche du temps perdu*. Marcel, however, has to go through the ordeals of the better part of a lifetime before he achieves the necessary conditioning for true artistic maturity. Marcel's first fulfilling account of writing is given in *Du Côté de chez Swann* as he rides in Dr. Percepied's carriage, but his aspirations to a literary career will also be marked by numerous setbacks. The experience of viewing the ever shifting perspective of the three steeples is almost meditative for it holds a sense of revelation suspending time and space which is an inherent part of the creative process. In *Du Côté de chez Swann*, this experience is surpassed only by the tea and madeleine incident which is referred to both directly and indirectly throughout the novel.

The role of art is manifest in the contrasting approaches to it by Swann and Marcel who, in a way, represent opposite sides of Proust's own personality. They represent, first in Swann, the side of the socialite and dilettante which marked Proust's earlier years and, secondly in Marcel, the side of the solitary reflective thinker and pursuer of artistic revelation which marked his later years. Swann tends to occupy himself with superficial pursuits amongst social climbers and idle aristocrats, promising himself that he will write a monograph on Vermeer, a promise he never fulfills. Conversely, Marcel resolves to write and, despite his setbacks, finally attains the exuberance of spirit necessary to the artist's goal. Swann belongs to a world bound by chronological time; Marcel belongs to one liberated from time itself.

The Tea and Madeleine Incident: If any sequence in *À La Recherche du temps perdu (Remembrance of Things Past)* could be set off as the master sequence of the work, then indeed the event depicting Marcel dipping his mother's madeleine into a cup of tea on a cold day could surely be isolated in this manner. The incident is alluded to often, and its transcendent experience even recurs in different guises as the novel cycle progresses. Its analogue in Marcel's far distant and seemingly forgotten past is his Aunt Léonie's giving him a similar treat on a Sunday morning before Mass. The transcendence and mystical beauty of the experience which brings with it the promise of everlasting childhood seems related also to the religious celebration and the actual consecrated Presence implicit therein, for we observe a reverent vision of Marcel partaking of elements vaguely resembling wine and bread, and he is granted a kind of taste of eternity. The resurrection **theme** becomes more obvious as the triadic structure of *À la Recherche du temps perdu* progresses, but even at this early point we may observe that Marcel's past visits to Combray occurred during Eastertide with its promise of spring and new eternal life. Many critics make a mistake in attempting to completely isolate the tea and madeleine sequence for they tend to lose sight of the fact that, as Marcel's cake was suffused in tea, the whole novel is suffused in the unwilled experience of meditation or involuntary memory of which the reflections of Reality are part of the creative process. The incident itself, along with the magic lantern reflections, seem to mark the genesis of creativity and artistic perception in Marcel.

CHARACTERIZATION IN DU CÔTÉ DE CHEZ SWANN (SWANN'S WAY): METHODS OF PORTRAYAL:

Most of the characters of primary significance to the development of the entire *À la Recherche du temps perdu* are introduced in *Du Côté de chez Swann* as many of its **themes** are likewise introduced in "Overture," its first section. The manner, however, in which the characters are introduced is significant if we are interested in their subsequent mutations. Following are simple descriptions of basic portrayal techniques of major Proustian characters, as they appear in *Du Côté de chez Swann*.

Marcel: Much has been noted in other sections concerning Marcel, but it also bears mentioning that Marcel is a first person "I" narrator and that the entire novel cycle is limited to his consciousness, with the exception of the "Un Amour de Swann" novella. In novels of great length, some critics and authors prefer omniscient narrative technique as the latter gives an author a greater degree of consciousness-latitude in terms of inter-character mobility, as it allows him to easily shift from the consciousness of one character to that of another. The omniscient technique, being a detached narrative technique rather than a primarily subjective one, often takes its toll in the personal intensity of the main character. Omniscient technique is frequently best suited for novels containing an overtly heavy and externally manifest plot line, such as one would find in the fiction of the Realists and Naturalists. The inception, however, of artist predicament novels in the twentieth century, with their essential abandonment of the objectified plot and detached characterizations, gave a new place to the first person narrative forms of "interior monologue" and "stream of consciousness." There are evidences of early beginnings of such techniques in Flaubert's incipient "internal monologue" crossed into third-person narrative, and in the work of Alain-Fournier. This direction in narration is continued through Proust who brought it into the foreground, and matures into radical "stream of consciousness" in such writers as Joyce, Woolf, and Faulkner. Basically, what the character of Marcel portrays in *Du Côté de chez Swann (Swann's Way)* is a young boy's idealized vision of the world as contrasted with the mature retrospective vision.

Swann: Mention has already been made of Swann's relationship to Odette, to art, and to Marcel, as well as his role of third-person narrator of "Un Amour de Swann." He becomes a highly important structural link in the cycle, and he basically portrays a projection of the artistically uncommitted and worldly young Proust. Swann's name holds a great fascination for Marcel, and he is to become as almost a mentor to Marcel in art appreciation. Swann sees nearly everything and everybody in terms of some painting. While Swann does not actually undergo mutation in the striking way some of the Proustian entourage does, we do learn that Swann has another life beyond the middleclass milieu of Combray. It is interesting, too, that he is a basically genteel, kindly person who does not arouse feelings of anti-Semitism in the community. The fact that he is the Jewish son of a wealthy stockbroker, in fact, points to his superior intelligence for, in spite of this social strike against him in a gentile milieu, he ascends the social hierarchy and sidesteps snob stigmas with a skill that makes the Verdurins look like babbling, muddleheaded fools.

Odette De Crecy: This character mutates in an astonishing way. In *Du Côté de chez Swann (Swann's Way)*, we unconsciously see her in the preliminary guise of Adolphe's "dame en rose" and, shortly following, as Elstir's "Miss Scaripant." She then appears as the socially stigmatized mistress of Swann, eventually giving to Tansonville its status as forbidden territory to Marcel's family. Odette is actually a very commonplace person - vulgar, superficial, mercenary. Swann, at first, sees her for what she is, but in his imagination he views her as an embodiment of abstract beauty. She emerges as an idealized example of young womanhood. She is able to deceive Swann in such a way that he pursues her all the more passionately, suffering all the agonies of the jealous lover. He even reads her mail and prowls about her window, checking to make sure she has no other callers. Her marriage to Swann and her contacts with the vulgar pseudo-noble follower in the Verdurin circle, M. de Forcheville, prefigure nevertheless her own and her daughter Gilberte's ascendancy to aristocratic circles. As is the case in many of Proust's characters who are viewed by Swann, Odette is portrayed as bearing likeness to works of art, in her case to Botticelli's Zipporah, Jethro's daughter, in the Sistine fresco. At the end of *Du Côté de chez Swann (Swann's Way)* the shadow of Gomorrah is cast over Odette in an anonymous letter sent to Swann.

Gilberte Swann: She appears in Marcel's first alluring glimpses through the beautiful yet thorny hawthorn boughs of the Tansonville hedge, and appears at first encounter as merely a childhood playmate in the Champs-Élysées.

Françoise: The servant of Marcel's family who is eventually to become his own housekeeper is portrayed in "pastiche" technique to bring out the humorous quality of her quaintly traditional speech mannerisms. She is a veritable member of the family and dominates the subordinate servants with whom her medieval traditionalism is sharply contrasted. Her personality, however, also has its negative side as can be seen in *Du Côté de chez Swann (Swann's Way)* in her cruelty in two specific instances: one involving a young unwed mother-to-be upon whom she prevails in the kitchen to cut asparagus to which the unfortunate girl is allergic, and the other involving her unrelenting manner of butchering a chicken in preparation for a particular meal. Art figures in the portrayal of a kitchen maid in terms of Swann's vision of Giotto's "Charity." Françoise's personal taste for reading and quoting Mme. de Sévigné also figures in her portrayal, as is the case in the portrayals of Aunt Léonie and Marcel's grandmother.

Aunt Léonie: The interesting part of her portrayal as a flighty hypochrondriac is the fact that Marcel, who finds her ways amusing, is to assume many of these same ways himself. She is portrayed with a great economy of strokes because the house and town with which she is identified are described at great length. Her presence pervades the tea and madeleine sequence, and she is a traditional admirer of Mme. de Sévigné's memoirs.

Marcel's Grandmother: She portrays the epitome of gentility and affectionate kindness. It will become increasingly more noticeable that she will be portrayed as admiring de Sévigné, for after her death, Marcel's mother will take on this element of the grandmother's tastes in an unconscious effort to preserve her presence. She is part of the general backdrop of *Du Côté de chez Swann (Swann's Way)* but assumes highly prominent roles in subsequent novels.

Mme. Verdurin: The tyrannical hostess of the Verdurin salon is portrayed as a socially self-conscious hypocrite, partly through "pastiche" technique parodying her stereotype qualities. Proust also recounts serious episodes involving her cruel snobbery and hypocrisy. Her simple-minded tastes are revealed when we learn of her unleashed, sustained peals of hysterical laughter upon hearing her protege Dr. Cottard's terrible puns which, in fact, had brought her to such wide-mouthed gales that she had to subsequently feign the gymnastic side of her hilarity on account of having at one time drawn her jaw out of joint. She is also given to feigning hypocritical laughter at things that she does not consider altogether funny. Her hypocrisy reaches full fruition when her obvious envy for higher social echelons surfaces despite her denigrations of them as "bores" and "idlers." She, in fact, becomes contemptuous of Swann when she suspects that he has social contacts with nobility and royalty whose hospitality he refuses to betray and ridicule. It is in the Verdurin circle that Swann is introduced to Odette, and it is here also that we catch our first glimpses of the future artist figures. The **theme** of "snobisme" relating to Mme. Verdurin, however, becomes increasingly preeminent as we leave *Du Côté de chez Swann (Swann's Way)* and observe her envy of the Guermantes and her ultimate penetration of their decadent circle. Comments regarding the forthcoming transformations of other seemingly obsequious members of the Verdurin circle who are eventually to come into their own artistically (or scientifically) can be noted in the segments on M. Vinteuil, Bergotte, Elstir, and Dr. Cottard elsewhere in this commentary.

Bloch: Comment has already been made upon Bloch as an unassimilated Jew. He has a monumental inferiority complex and anti-Semitism is not the reason for Marcel's family's disapproval of him. He is portrayed as resembling Mohamet II. Marcel, in his company, has an encounter with a girl who is later introduced to him by Saint Loup as Rachel. Eventually, Bloch is to become a successful playwright, but his primary significance in *Du Côté de chez Swann (Swann' Way)* lies in the fact that he lends Marcel a book by Bergotte and introduces Marcel to a character from low life who will later appear with an aristocrat.

The Baron De Charlus: In *Du Côté de chez Swann (Swann's Way)*, Marcel has not as yet personally met this man and does not yet understand the sinister aspects of his countenance, but some subtle hints are dropped concerning him which are to prepare us for his later emergence as a fully developed character. One such hint is that suggested by Swann implying that his presence at Tansonville poses no threat to the virtue of Odette or Gilberte. Otherwise, he appears innocuously as a somewhat formidable middle-aged man. Little do we realize that there is to be an insidious link between Marcel's viewing of the incident at Montjouvain and the ensuing plunge into the nether world of *Sodome et Gomorrhe*. It will not be until *Le Côté de Guermantes (The Guermantes Way)* that we will discover the extent and viciousness of de Charlus' snobbery, especially that toward Jews.

Mlle. Vinteuil: In a way, she is the most frightening character encountered in the otherwise idyllic *Du Côté de chez Swann (Swann's Way)*. Obviously having a severe psychiatric problem, she is depicted as the mannish woman who is viewed by the young Marcel as she engages in a secret affair and in a ritual of paternal profanation. The wretched scene serves a structural purpose in the novel, for it follows closely after a magnificent description of passing lilac blossoms and serves to prefigure Marcel's coming into a quite unidealized world. The incident carries an impact in a much later section of the cycle as well, for Albertine will innocently refer to Mlle. Vinteuil in an effort to project an impression of familiarity with musical people. It will draw us back to the Montjouvain incident with the impact of a Classical recognition scene.

PREEMINENT IMAGERY IN DU CÔTÉ DE CHEZ SWANN (SWANN'S WAY)

Brief comment may be made at this point on the primary images in the first novel although more specific detail will appear after the entire cycle is examined. The following images emerge in the work to become prominently recurring motifs.

There is a profusion of images associated with the subject matter at the very beginning of the work: sleep, dreams, and waking. Associated with this image-laden material are those connected with windows, light, shadow, and bedrooms in general. As in works by Franz Kafka such as "The Metamorphosis" and *The Trial*, we come out of a vast realm of sleep into a waking world even more vast and dreamlike. Likewise, Proust begins his cycle with the thematic material associated with sleep, dreams, and waking.

Proust's most vivid images are those involving the play of vision, light, and color, of which some of the most memorable include the images of the kaleidoscope, the magic lantern, and stained glass windows. Marcel, who so strongly identifies with traditional pastoral France, finds the historical portrayals of Golo and Genevieve de Brabant fascinating and endearing. This also links to Marcel's attraction toward country churches, of which the Combray church and the visionary one of Balbec occupy his mind. Golo pursuing Genevieve also introduces the **theme** of the chase and the captive which materializes to full strength in Marcel's relationship with Albertine.

Imagery dealing with scientific instruments used for diagnosing illness becomes prominent in passages relating to the love, jealousy, disillusionment thematology. One may observe this in a particularly striking way in "Un Amour de Swann" where Charles Swann's love relationship is frequently recounted in terms of its being a serious illness. Among the instruments of diagnosis alluded to are any number of optical instruments and their properties of focusing, magnifying, refraction, and deflection. One can observe all sorts of references to lenses, glasses, windows and kaleidoscopes in the novel. Because the faculty of sight most readily defies analysis, its manifestations and illusions serve well in relating intuitive processes. Oftentimes other sense perceptions, such as those relating to musical sounds, will be related in the synaesthetic **imagery** of visual effects.

Amid the fascinating array of botanical images that one may find in Proust is the colorful floral **imagery** associated with specific characters, places, and events. The orchid becomes the image primarily associated with Odette, and it may be rooted back to Swann's adjusting a cattelya orchid on Odette's dress as they roll along in a carriage. The expression "faire cattelya" becomes part of the personal parlance of the couple in the early stages of their love affair and gives orchids part of their symbolic value. Later, one observes more sinister undertones in orchid **imagery** when it becomes connected with the bumblebee image. The chrysanthemum is also an image associated with Odette, for Swann had taken a chrysanthemum blossom and had hidden it away in his desk as a memento of Odette.

As hawthorns and lilacs are images associated with the Méséglise Way, pond lillies become integrally associated with the Guermantes Way. One of Proust's most outstanding floral passages is the one describing the dying lilacs just prior to the recounting of the Montjouvain sequence. However, the most beautiful of the passages containing floral **imagery** are those focusing on the pink hawthorns. One views these delicate spring flowers with their fragile knob-like clusters of tiny, perfectly detailed petals on the altar of the Combray church, in a hedge of high shrubs around Tansonville, and in the mind and memories of Marcel. The recurring hawthorn image moves through *Du Côté de chez Swann (Swann's Way)* and reappears in other novels of the cycle as well. Marcel's contemplation of hawthorns in and of themselves, and in the context of their later connection with Gilberte, carries an impact transcending time. They also figure in a powerful involuntary memory sequence in *À l'Ombre des jeunes filles en fleurs (Within a Budding Grove)*.

Among the other organic images, the zoological also figure in Proust's personifications and motifs, among the most important of which are the ornithological images. These images of bird figures are prominent in the descriptions of such socialites as the Guermantes, and in the imagery relating to the music of Chopin at Mme. Saint-Euverte's musicale. Particularly memorable although less pleasant is the fowl **imagery** of two repugnant, clucking chickens romping about in the window scene at Montjouvain.

SOCIAL EVENTS IN DU CÔTÉ DE CHEZ SWANN (SWANN'S WAY)

In examining the parties and musicales at which numerous Proustian characters gather throughout *À la Recherche du temps perdu (Remembrance of Things Past)*, two primary factors are to be observed: one is that we ascend the ladder of social prominence with each social event that is presented, and the other is that they become longer in their page consumption as the novel progresses from the idyllic inner subjective world of Marcel to the quagmire of worldly competition and doomed social enterprise.

In understanding the nature of these social gatherings, we must realize the significance of the salon in traditional French life. There is no exact counterpart in the Anglo-Saxon heritage that possesses the regal prominence of the elegant Parisian salons. Not only were the salons of social significance as any exclusive person's home or parlor might be, but they were actually places of intellectual ferment at which daring new works of art and music were presented to the influential elite who could subsequently affect an artist's exposure, reputation, and progress. The British coffee houses and drawing rooms bore a resemblance to the French salons, but did not have the exclusivity and regal status of the salons. Perhaps the phenomenon still extant today in the U.S. most closely resembling a salon gathering is the sort of opening night exhibitions and performances which some of the more exclusive museums have open only to their members. Even though this sort of elitist activity has largely disappeared amid our mass culture, small pockets of it still exist in museum openings, and in private showings and concerts at college alumni functions. At such events, not only is the art of importance to the guests but the dining, mingling, and social climbing are as well. The French salons were presided over by prominent aristocratic ladies who acted as gracious hostesses amid plush surroundings to their distinguished guests. The feminine element was, of course, prevalent and often overpowering in the salons, as contrasted with the masculine orientation of the English coffee houses. The guests constituted the most influential persons of powerful cliques and the membership of a salon was a tight closed group. Proust portrays these closed groups in a succession of lavish entertainments which take us upward from the cliques of one social plateau to those of higher, more exclusive plateaus. In *Du Côté de chez Swann (Swann's Way)*, there are three social events which are presented in colorful and resplendent detail. The first two take place at the salon of Mme. Verdurin which, status-wise, is at the bottom of the social climber's ladder. The third takes place at the estate of a minor aristocratic figure, Mme. de Saint-Euverte.

MOMENTS OF HEIGHTENED CONSCIOUSNESS IN DU CÔTÉ DE CHEZ SWANN (SWANN'S WAY)

The tea and madeleine sequence: Much comment has already been made upon this occurrence, but one should bear in mind specifically what such moments portend in the context of the novel cycle of *À la Recherche du temps perdu (Remembrance of Things Past)* as a whole. The recollective impact of the exquisite shudder incurred by this simple treat on a cold morning is of seismographic proportions, for it not only brings us the psychological and sociological totality of Combray, but it launches the entire Proustian cycle. It sets forces of both anticipation and recollection in motion and prefigures other moments of involuntary memory.

The Steeples of Martinville sequence: Not only is the spacious view of the ever shifting perspective of the three steeples significant to Marcel's vocation as a writer in inspiring him to write his first fulfilling little fragment, but they give him an awareness of more profound sense of reality than that which meets the eye. The uncrowded freedom of the wind-swept and sunlit ride gives Marcel's mind the kind of free rein that makes it responsive to the fluid preciousness of three steeples which give the illusion of themselves moving, changing in perspective to one-another as well as to the onlooker, and transcending the ordinary realms of time and space. This scene is primarily anticipatory rather than recollective, for we realize similarities between it and later sequences. One later sequence resembling the three steeples sequence appears in *À l'Ombre des jeunes filles en fleurs (Within a Budding Grove)* and relates Marcel's chance viewing of three trees at Hudimesnil near Balbec from Mme. de Villeparisis' carriage. It also anticipates an incipient revelation in *Le Temps retrouvé (The Past Recaptured)* as a depressed Marcel looks out the window of a train and sees sunlight upon a row of trees.

À L'OMBRE DES JEUNES FILLES EN FLEURS (WITHIN A BUDDING GROVE): PUBLISHING HISTORY AND GENERAL INTRODUCTION

The second novel of Proust's cycle was published in 1918 after delays in publishing incurred by World War I. Like *Du Côté de chez Swann (Swann's Way)* and several of the other novels of the cycle, this one was actually published in two volumes. It concerns itself primarily with events in Paris and with Marcel's first trip to Balbec with his grandmother. Proust was awarded the Goncourt Prize for *À l'Ombre des jeunes filles en fleurs* in 1919, gaining immediate literary fame, and gaining recognition at last for *Du Côté de chez Swann*. Unfortunately, Proust was not to enjoy fame for long, for he was to live only until 1922. There is a sad but beautifully wrought **theme** of disillusionment which runs through the second novel, and there is no ebb in the exuberance of Proust's brilliant writing in this book.

PLOT SUMMARY OF À L'OMBRE DES JEUNES FILLES EN FLEURS (WITHIN A BUDDING GROVE)*

The second novel follows Swann and Odette after their marriage, and presents Marcel as an adolescent who is still in love with his childhood playmate, Gilberte, who is viewed recurrently through the Tansonville hawthorns. Gilberte's parents become attached to Marcel, but she becomes bored with him for his hypochrondriacal ways. Marcel has, however, been able to meet the writer Bergotte through Gilberte. Marcel, disappointed, sees La Berma in his first direct experience with the arts. We become aware of bitter political polarization over the Dreyfus Case.

For his health, Swann suggests that Marcel go to Balbec. He goes there with his grandmother where at the Grand Hôtel they meet his grandmother's school friend, Mme. de Villeparisis, a Guermantes, who is visited by her soldier nephew stationed at Doncières. Marcel and Saint Loup become close friends. Saint Loup is in a love subplot with the Jewish actress Rachel. Marcel also meets the Baron de Charlus (Saint Loup's uncle and the younger brother of Duc de Guermantes) for the first time at Balbec. Marcel meets Elstir with Saint Loup and they visit his studio.

---

* Permission for plot summaries and quotations has been granted by Random House, Inc., and Alfred A. Knopf, Inc.

The primary event is the emergence of Albertine Simonet, at first anonymous in a group of girls, but to be introduced by Elstir and to become Marcel's love. She symbolizes the freshness and idealized vitality of youth. The novel ends in a mood of disillusionment as autumn descends on an increasingly vacated Balbec. Marcel's grandmother is photographed in a **foreshadowing** of her impending death.

MAJOR STRUCTURAL AND THEMATIC ELEMENTS IN À L'OMBRE DES JEUNES FILLES EN FLEURS (WITHIN A BUDDING GROVE)

The conclusion of *Du Côté de chez Swann (Swann's Way)* prepares us for one of the major sections of the following novel by suggesting that there is some immanent significance to the name "Balbec" in "Place Names: the Name." The full Balbec sequence does not come, however, until the second half of the novel, the first half dealing generally with events in Paris. Thematically, much of the structural material introduced in *Du Côté de chez Swann (Swann's Way)* is sustained with some variations on a **theme** in *À l'Ombre des jeunes filles en fleurs (Within a Budding Grove)*. Of primary significance are the **themes** of Marcel's "invisible vocation," disillusionment, and "déclassement." New thematic material introduced in the second novel is that pertaining to Elstir's vision as a seascape artist, and the **theme** of death with the grandmother in its ominous shadow. The **themes** of Marcel's capacity for heightened awareness through contemplation and through involuntary memory are also prominent in *À l'Ombre des jeunes filles en fleurs*. Of preeminent significance in this and the succeeding novels of the cycle, however, is the portrayal of both the familiar and the new characters. The mutations and recurrences of the characters established in *Du Côté de chez Swann (Swann's Way)* provide a unique fascination for the

Proustian reader and are often the lure to reading the voluminous cycle in its entirety. Interaction between the familiar and new characters also provides excitement for the reader and adds new thrust to the plot line. An example of such an interesting play with the characters in this book is the new focus on Marcel's father, who seems a very distant paternal figure in *Du Côté de chez Swann*. We see considerably more of Marcel's mother in the cycle, and she eclipses the father almost totally in the first novel. The main reason for this is the fact that Marcel is psychologically closer to his mother, and the novel's fictional technique presents the narrative through the subjective consciousness of Marcel. Proust himself was considerably closer to his mother than to his father, and Marcel seems as a projection of the author. Some critics believe that Proust felt like an inferior weakling before his prominent and successful father, and believe that Proust deemphasized the father figure in his cycle for this reason. It is also conspicuous that the younger brother figure has been eliminated entirely and that a dislike for doctors and diplomats persists.

THEME OF MARCEL'S VOCATION AS A WRITER

This **theme** is continued in *À l'Ombre des jeunes filles en fleurs (Within a Budding Grove)* in two sequences of the novel, one of which is seemingly a blatant, socially-oriented digression, but crucial, nevertheless, to the development of the work as a whole, and the other of which is a subtle contemplation evocative of Marcel's vision of the three steeples. In the beginning, Marcel's gradual growth to artistic maturity suffers from an inevitable setback when M. de Norpois, a respected friend of Marcel's father, scathes his work and ridicules his idolized Bergotte. As we become exposed to M. de Norpois, we learn to discount his literary judgments as pretentious pseudo-intellectual babble. Marcel, however, as a yet naive boy is upset by Norpois' former enthusiasm turning unaccountably and abruptly to scorn. By contrast with the egocentric M. de Norpois, Bergotte and Elstir are shortly to become Marcel's acquaintances.

THEME OF "SNOBISME"

The interaction of literary opinions during Mme. Swann's dinner party serves not only to place the young Marcel in perspective in the second novel, but serves also to reveal the hollowness and snobbery of M. de Norpois and the facility with which Marcel's father falls for his pretentious officiality. Each of the men is a part of the pretentious facade of governmental diplomacy. Other contacts with snob elements in this novel include Mme. de Villeparisis who even speaks down to her own aristocratic relatives, Robert de Saint Loup and the Baron de Charlus. We are interested, also, in the degree of social protocol necessary in entering the closed family and salon circles. Marcel must await formal introduction to Gilberte before approaching her, anticipating that de Norpois will intercede for him. We notice even in Balbec a hierarchy in the exclusivity of the villages, reminding us in a way of the villages of Cape Cod.

Closely related to the **theme** of "snobisme" is that of the Dreyfus Affair and its reception in polite society. Marcel, like his family, leans toward the liberal Dreyfusards. We shall discover in this and the two succeeding novels, *Le Côté de Guermantes* and *Sodome et Gomorrhe*, that most of the aristocratic circle and its followers are anti-Dreyfusards simply out of a sense of conformity. The role of the Jews in a mercurial, kaleidoscopic society of flux and change is preeminent in Proustian literature.

DISILLUSIONMENT

The pervading atmosphere of *À l'Ombre des jeunes filles en fleurs (Within a Budding Grove)* is one of disillusionment, but among the greater specific disillusionments of Marcel are his disappointment in his visit to the theatre, in his first meeting with Bergotte, in seeing Balbec and its church for the first time, in learning through Elstir that Albertine comes from a very ordinary background, in seeing Albertine up close for the first time, and in discovering that the Elstir of the beautiful seascapes is actually the Master Biche of former days. Marcel is afflicted with a disillusionment syndrome rooted in his creativity and inherent inclination to build idealized pictures of things, which in ordinary reality, lack this extra visionary dimension. His sense of anticipation is overwrought and dreamlike, as in the cases of his expectations concerning La Berma and the "Persian" church at Balbec.

ART

Such material on the arts as the passage on Mme. Swann's playing of the Vinteuil sonata, the **allusions** made to Vermeer, and the recurrence of the magic lantern motif, is material extended out of *Du Côté de chez Swann (Swann's Way)*. There are also extensions of material in the first novel which introduced La Berma by references to her distinguished name, and familiarized us with the technique of Bergotte. La Berma's art emerges as embodying Racine to perfection, and Bergotte's as brilliantly transforming objects in terms of their inner realities. *À l'Ombre des jeunes filles en fleurs (Within a Budding Grove)* also presents a brilliant, extended passage relating to Elstir's artistic vision as we visit his studio with the metaphorically responsive Marcel. This section of *À l'Ombre des jeunes filles en fleurs* stands out as superlative literature along with the moments of involuntary memory and heightened consciousness.

DEATH

This **theme** emerges at three strategic points in the novel of which one is the passing remark that Aunt Léonie has died, but of which the other two are premonitory sequences anticipating the death of Marcel's grandmother. One is an experience of involuntary memory in a Champs-Élysées lavatory pavilion, and the other is the sequence in which the grandmother insists that Robert de Saint Loup take her picture as promptly as possible. We are to learn later of her illness which will strike its final blow in the Champs Élysées in *Le Côté de Guermantes (The Guermantes Way)* and that the picture was intended as a posthumous keepsake for the grandson - a photograph of her before the inevitable ravages of stroke and final illness were to set in. The onslaught of autumn in Balbec is subtly anticipatory of impending death as well. We note particularly the yellowish colorations which exude from the autumnal sunlit surfaces, vaguely anticipatory of Bergotte's death vision of Vermeer's spot of sunlit yellow wall in his view of the Dutch town of Delft following a storm.

CHARACTERIZATION IN À L'OMBRE DES JEUNES FILLES EN FLEURS (WITHIN A BUDDING GROVE): METHODS OF PORTRAYAL

Marcel: The portrayal of the narrator continues with consistency from the first novel although he is now portrayed as an adolescent. He is, nevertheless, to remain under the influence of his parents and their friends. Focus is continually placed on his keen mental responsiveness to art, literature, and music, and he continues to experience deliverances in the heightened consciousness of contemplation and involuntary memory.

Marcel's Father: He emerges from being a background figure and is portrayed as a conscientious man of professional standing in the diplomatic service. His traditionalism in matters relating to the arts is revealed in his hesitation in completely approving of Marcel's pursuing a literary career and in his reluctance over allowing him to attend a theatre performance. The mother figure will shrink in this novel as Marcel will be traveling to Balbec with his grandmother and will be away from his mother for the first time.

Swann: The friend of Marcel's family, while still very similar in portrayal here as in the first novel, emerges as a more aggressive social climber than before. The lure of Gilberte draws Marcel to them, and it is by an accident of circumstance that he is introduced to the family on an adult level. Regarding Odette, we are to discover that she was the "Miss Scaripant" of former days.

Gilberte: The daughter of Swann becomes the object of Marcel's brief love and inevitable jealousy during the first half of *A l'Ombre de jeunes filles en fleurs (Within a Budding Grove)*. She is portrayed as worldly and as consequently becoming quickly bored with the introspective and hypochondriacal Marcel.

Dr. Cottard: He remains very much as he had been in the first novel amid the Verdurin "clan," being primarily a social dullard. However, distinction is made between his social self and his considerably more astute professional self. A social blunder of his accidentally brings Marcel to a formal introduction into the Swann household and thus brings Marcel and Gilberte together.

Dr. Cottard, however, is to undergo more change. One of the most memorable passages in *À l'Ombre des jeunes filles en fleurs (Within a Budding Grove)* is that on men changing to their exact opposites.

Bergotte: The author becomes more significant by the second novel. His acceptance in the circle of Marcel's family is actually amusing, for their disapproval of this offbeat and arty individual is dispelled by Bergotte's compliments of their son's talents. The author is portrayed as the antithesis of M. de Norpois, having reciprocal dislike and scorn for the continually talking, pretentious dilettante.

M. De Norpois: In terms of character portrayal, M. de Norpois is presented more masterfully than any of the other figures in *À l'Ombre des jeunes filles en fleurs (Within a Budding Grove)*. He is a new character entered into the cycle and strikes us full force at the beginning of this novel, being portrayed in scathing "pastiche" as he emerges in farcical conversation with Marcel and his father. De Norpois is the hopeless victim of **cliches** and inane stock phrases as Dr. Cottard is with bad puns. An inveterate, overly talkative snob, he lends himself perfectly to caricature. Proust himself was encouraged to enter the government service, and his inevitable encounters with egocentric diplomats like de Norpois no doubt gave him his contempt for them. The stuffy diplomat considers himself indispensable to his country and considers Marcel's attempts at writing to be foolishness. He had first encouraged Marcel in writing and theatregoing, but upon discovering that Marcel's work rings of "Art for Art's Sake," he is reminded of Bergotte and immediately turns against the whole idea with a volley of innuendo, insult, and ridicule.

Elstir: By this novel, he has broken from the Verdurin mold and has come into his own as an established Impressionist artist, having discovered his "thing" in interpretations of the sea.

Marcel meets him with Robert de Saint Loup at Rivebelle, and at his grandmother's suggestion, accepts the invitation to Elstir's studio. The artist is portrayed as generous in spirit, giving of himself in his artistic creations, and giving of himself in his hospitable introduction of Marcel to Albertine and the "band."

Albertine: Like Odette and Gilberte, Albertine emerges in idealized form from a group. At first, Marcel's contemplation of the "little band" was so great that it delayed his visit to Elstir, but eventually even kissing Albertine is a disappointment to Marcel.

Saint Loup: He is a handsome young man who becomes Marcel's close friend despite his initial appearance of snobbishness. He will undergo a process of mutation in the later novels of the cycle.

Marcel's Grandmother: She is portrayed as a mother substitute for Marcel at Balbec. She is dignified, reserved and secretive about her illness.

The Baron De Charlus: Marcel meets him for the first time on a walk with his grandmother and Mme. de Villeparisis but is puzzled by his strange, temperamental demeanor.

Mme. De Villeparisis: She is portrayed as the primary link between Marcel and the Guermantes, Robert de Saint Loup and the Baron de Charlus, whom she treats with condescension.

IMAGERY IN À L'OMBRE DES JEUNES FILLES EN FLEURS (WITHIN A BUDDING GROVE)

In the succession of novels in *À la Recherche du temps perdu*, we shall note a sharp decline in the profusion and richness of the

imagery as we enter the social world and the **themes** associated with it. There are, nevertheless, numerous fine examples of **imagery** in *À l'Ombre des jeunes filles en fleurs*.

The floral images are among the finest, as in the recurrence of the hawthorn image which reminds us of Combray and Gilberte. Rose imagery appears in references to adolescence and in the anticipation of Albertine's kiss. Odette is surrounded by flowers in her home and even elderly ladies are described in botanical **imagery**. Vinteuil's music is, of course, described with images although not with the exuberance of the descriptions in *Du Côté de chez Swann (Swann's Way)*. Marine **imagery** becomes preeminent with the introduction of the Balbec resort and it tends to supersede the floral **imagery**. Albertine's "little band" is likened to seagulls, and numerous references to strange fish and other aquatic creatures are made amid the sense of fluidity of the water. The play of optical illusion is presented with Marcel's first close-up glimpse of Albertine upon meeting her, as well as in the delusion which the grandmother triumphantly preserves in her photograph. A superlative image relating to the **theme** of "snobisme" is that of Mme. de Villeparisis beholding Robert de Saint Loup and the Baron de Charlus as one would look at creatures in a zoo.

MOMENTS OF HEIGHTENED CONSCIOUSNESS IN À L'OMBRE DES JEUNES FILLES EN FLEURS (WITHIN A BUDDING GROVE)

An involuntary memory sequence involving a peculiar musty odor in a Champs-Élysées pavilion brings to Marcel recollections of Uncle Adolphe's room which bore a similar scent. It is also vaguely reminiscent of the smell of orris root which filled an outbuilding prominent in Marcel's distant solitary memories.

Most significantly, this experience in the Champs-Élysées is premonitory of Marcel's grandmother's death which will take place in *Le Côté de Guermantes (The Guermantes Way)*, covering many of its latter pages.

There is an incipient involuntary memory sequence involving three trees viewed at Hudimesnil from Mme. de Villeparisis' carriage. They evoke the responsive chords of memory, and while Marcel cannot exactly identify the memory triggered, there is an obvious link between the trees and the three steeples.

A hedge of flowerless hawthorns at Balbec brings back a flood of precious childhood memories of Combray. The vision is sadly indicative of passing time for the beautiful flowers are gone from the scaly, prickly stems, and Marcel is reminded of the Combray hawthorns in full idyllic bloom.

LE CÔTÉ DE GUERMANTES (THE GUERMANTES WAY): PUBLISHING HISTORY AND GENERAL INTRODUCTION

The two volumes of *Le Côté de Guermantes* were published in 1920 and won world-wide fame for the author. As we approach the center of the seven-novel cycle, the emphasis upon the transitory, time-imbued world of society becomes increasingly great as the focus centers upon the social circles of the Guermantes, giving emphasis to Proust's vision of "memoirs of Saint-Simon of another period." We see the splendor of the Faubourg Saint-Germain, but we see it also as a place of frustrated hopes and lost illusions. Society, friendship, and even love turn out to be frauds: people and things lack permanence. This will give further impact at the end of the cycle to Marcel's discovery of the only things that survive and remain intact: the great works of art in the world which includes Vinteuil's brilliant yet sad music.

PLOT SUMMARY OF LE CÔTÉ DE GUERMANTES (THE GUERMANTES WAY)*

This novel finds Marcel living in Paris in an apartment in the Hôtel de Guermantes rented by his parents. Here, Marcel dreams of coming into social contact with the Duchesse whom he had seen and admired from a distant view as a child, but as her tenant, he is not in her social echelon which he so longs to penetrate. Marcel is finally invited to her salon and presented to her, but only through connections with Mme. de Villeparisis, the Baron de Charlus, and Robert de Saint Loup. Marcel becomes solidly established in the Guermantes circle but comes to be disillusioned with it. The Duchesse de Guermantes is cruel and calculating, and the Baron de Charlus has a severe psychiatric problem.

We see in excruciating detail the death of Marcel's grandmother, a terrible blow from which Marcel makes only a gradual recovery. After her death, Marcel's mother returns to Combray, leaving Marcel under the care of Françoise who promptly alienates Albertine for her disapproval of her visiting Marcel and staying with him unchaperoned.

We learn that Swann is seriously ill as Marcel meets him at the Guermantes' where Swann is now an unwelcome guest. As Swann comes to tell of his impending death to the Duc and Duchesse, she exhibits her shallow coldness by showing more

---

* Plot summaries are given by permission of Alfred A. Knopf, Inc., and Random House, Inc.

interest in her choice of party slippers than in a matter of life and death. The Duc cares not to admit that this will be a final visit.

THEMATIC STRUCTURAL ELEMENTS OF LE CÔTÉ DE GUERMANTES (THE GUERMANTES WAY)

An increasing predilection with the mundane world of society gives this novel a new heaviness and seriousness not yet encountered in the first two novels of the cycle. The humor becomes ominously dark in its satirical quality, particularly in its treatment of the pathetic sides of hypocrisy, bigotry and vice. We are introduced promptly to the salon of Mme. de Villeparisis and the description of the matinee takes up an unprecedented number of pages, to be surpassed only by the subsequent description in the second half of the novel of the Duchesse de Guermantes' dinner party, and by the segmental description of the Princesse de Guermantes' party in *Sodome et Gomorrhe (Cities of the Plain)*. The social encounters in *Le Côté de Guermantes (The Guermantes Way)* are manifold, but the three most significant ones are the formal occasion blocks: two parties given by Mme. de Villeparisis and one given by the Duchesse. Other social encounters include Marcel's visit to Robert de Saint Loup at Doncières, his bizarre visit to the Baron de Charlus, and his brief visit to the Duc and Duchesse at the novel's conclusion.

To say that that this novel exudes a feeling of disillusionment is a gross understatement: its overriding tone, especially in its second part, is one of the destructability of the transitory things with which society is obsessed and of the inevitability of death. In this way, we find ourselves in a plunge into the triadic cycle's death-center even before opening *Sodome et Gomorrhe*. Even the central **theme** of the novel is revealed throughout *Le Côté de Guermantes*, for a profusion of evidence of vice abounds in this work. The reason the reader is not directly involved in it is because the material is limited to Marcel's first-person narrative consciousness, and he is not as yet ready to find what actually surrounds him in almost full view. Marcel is still endowed with the vestiges of his childhood innocence and capacity for idealization, as is the case in his vision of the Duchesse before actually knowing her.

Theme of Social Stratification: The theme of "snobisme" is sustained in one way in this novel by the fact that, again, Marcel needs to be formally introduced to a person whose acquaintance he wishes to make despite the fact that, for instance, he and the Duchesse have seen and acknowledged one another. They belong to different social strata, and protocol demands formal introduction and presentation. Marcel, at this point, is only her tenant at the Hôtel de Guermantes, but his confirmed acquaintance with Mme. de Villeparisis and Robert de Saint Loup, along with neighborly encounters, prepares the long way for Marcel's eventual acceptance into the Duchesse's circle. Along the way in this ascendancy, the basic material with which *Le Côté de Guermantes (The Guermantes Way)* deals, Marcel hears the entire spectrum of remarks and opinions on the controversial Dreyfus Case from people ranging from butlers to nobility. This material on Dreyfusism contains some of Marcel Proust's finest **satire** and social commentary as well as bringing in a profusion of eccentric minor characters. Interestingly, the prominence of the Dreyfus Affair points to the mercurial, topsy-turvy aspect of social stratification, for at this particular time the kaleidoscope of flux and change has temporarily shifted the Jews to the bottom of the social hierarchy. The basic significance of the three major social events in this novel is their function of exposing intersecting views and rationales for pro- and anti-Dreyfusism.

Theme of Idealization and Disillusionment: As *Le Côté de Guermantes (The Guermantes Way)* opens, Marcel is still possessed by his subjective, imaginative view of the Duchesse de Guermantes. Her acknowledgments of him in public, such as her wave to him from a theatre box seat, serve only to tease and entice the naive Marcel, for it is not until very late in this novel that he actually receives an invitation from her to visit in her own place. His projected image of her is that of embodied elegance and regal grace. It is for a respite from his preoccupation with her that he visits Saint Loup at Doncières, only to find the Duchesse's presence there too in the form of a picture of her belonging to Saint Loup. Marcel has an imaginary view of her aristocratic way of life being somehow beyond the pale of the petty concerns of ordinary little human beings. Marcel is, however, only to discover that she is an egotistical, calculating shrew with a cruel husband who, together with her husband, fails to ever acknowledge impending death when its disregard for the social calendar threatens their activities.

Theme of "Déclassement": The Parisian world is still heavy laden under the yoke of social stratification and "snobisme" in this novel, but hints at its transparency are nevertheless made. Among the most striking of these are the remarks made about the general leveling off of the hierarchy in the army milieu of Doncières. Even Saint Loup himself has defied class boundaries by escorting a Jewish actress as a lover, not to mention the fact which Marcel himself discovers upon actually seeing her - the realization that Rachel, who heaps demands upon him, is the same girl that Marcel had glimpsed while visiting a house of ill fame during his acquaintance with Bloch in *Du Côté de chez Swann (Swann's Way)*. As the old conventional hierarchies of society begin to fall away, we anticipate in *Le Côté de Guermantes (The Guermantes Way)* the new hierarchies which are to come into full view in the following novel - the hidden hierarchies of vice, secret societies which include kings as well as servants. The shadow of *Sodome et Gomorrhe (Cities of the Plain)* looms heavily: hanging over Bloch and de Norpois as evidenced at Mme. de Villeparisis' first party, over Saint Loup despite his fury in a theatre, over Rachel in an invitation she extends to a dancer, and most obviously over the Baron de Charlus. The rancid odor of the cities of the plain emits from numerous characters, but most frighteningly from those who, like Saint Loup, we think we know but who mutate into various insidious psychological patterns.

Theme of Death: The material on this subject encompasses a vast portion of *Le Côté de Guermantes (The Guermantes Way)* taking numerous forms in the course of the work. One form which it takes is in introducing the telephone motif, a motif appearing in the following novel as well. Marcel places a telephone call to his grandmother from Doncières, but when he actually hears her voice after a delay at the Central Exchange, it seems to have a terrifying other-worldly quality. It has a strangely transparent purity and becomes a transcendent, disembodied reality far beyond her ordinary familiar face-to-face voice. Marcel, in fact, can scarcely recognize it as hers. When it suddenly stops, he frantically calls her name and at once departs for Paris. Marcel's experience upon his arrival at the house also prefigures the grandmother's death for when he enters the house, he finds a lady reading Mme. de Sévigné whom he scarcely recognizes. The grandmother is caught off guard and some extraordinary faculty in Marcel perceives the hidden secret of her heretofore undisclosed illness and imminent death. These events come early in the work and are followed by a third premonitory sequence about midway through in which Marcel experiences a premonition in the Champs-Élysées.

This death **theme** fills much of the latter part of *Le Côté de Guermantes (The Guermantes Way)* and the final illness and death of the grandmother, plus Bergotte's illness, fills pages of it. With the exception of the soiree of Mme. de Villeparisis, the rather lengthy dinner party of the Duchesse, and some material relating to the Prince, the Baron de Charlus, and Albertine, the entirety of the second half of this novel is concerned with death. We find ourselves in an abyss even before opening *Sodome et Gomorrhe (Cities of the Plain)* - the abyss of a decadent society and its obsessions with unauthentic, superficial things. **Foreshadowing** the end in which the Duc and Duchesse give priority to their selection of her slippers so as to avoid delay caused by speaking with Swann on a heavy subject, we find the terrible Professor E. refusing to pay a call to Marcel's grandmother because of a pressing need to have a coat altered for an upcoming social event. In each case, mundane concerns take precedence over matters of life and death.

Art: In *Le Côté de Guermantes (The Guermantes Way)*, the material on the arts is considerably less rich than in the two preceding novels. The reason for this lies in the basic thematology found in the center of the work: society, moral decay, death. It is basic to the triadic design of the cycle. There are, however, some scattered references to the arts which include some thoughts on the perfection of La Berma's Phaedra, the long delayed ascent of Renoir, and contemplation of the Elstirs at the Duchesse de Guermantes' home.

Marcel's Vocation: Only a small amount of material appears on this subject, for at this point Marcel is traversing his worldly phase. This will heighten the impact of his unexpected rediscovery of the eternity of art later. Marcel, however, is again reminded of his three steeples in a composite involuntary memory sequence in Paris while descending a staircase, and he later awaits the publication of a journal article. His attendance at the first Mme. de Villeparisis party was upon his father's suggestion, his hoping that M. de Norpois might again attempt to advise Marcel.

CHARACTERIZATION IN LE CÔTÉ DE GUERMANTES (THE GUERMANTES WAY): METHODS OF PORTRAYAL:

Marcel: The narrator is portrayed as still basically an idealist and is oblivious to things which are flagrantly apparent to the reader, such as the Baron de Charlus' intentions in approaching him. He is in raptures over the Duchesse and views Elstir's paintings with an intentness similar to that of Swann in listening to Vinteuil's music. Marcel loves his grandmother and suffers terribly upon losing her.

Marcel's Grandmother: She is portrayed through her illness as a person who wishes to spare others pain and so is secretive about the onslaught of her final illness and imminent death. In her trying to keep it from her grandson, it gathers unsurpassed intensity. She, like Bergotte who is also portrayed as seriously ill, will pass from this world in the full view of the reader. Most of the Proustian characters disappear "offstage," and we only hear of their passing, as is the case with Aunt Léonie, M. Swann, and Gilberte.

Mme. De Villeparisis: More remarks are made on her noble background but strange displacement from the inner Guermantes circle. Her first social event, like that of the Duchesse, covers a vast number of pages in which conversations primarily on the Dreyfus Case ensue.

The Duchesse De Guermantes: The focal point of her portrayal is the projection of her unpleasant qualities of which the purpose is to reveal through the narrator's consciousness the disparity between the idealized vision and the actual reality. Marcel's vision of her is finally broken by her emergence in reality as a cruel husband's wife who is full of malicious talk and who treats her servants badly. Like the hollow ground wit of the Baron de Charlus, that of the Duchesse is likewise stropped and honed on those about her. Her attitude toward the Elstir paintings simply places them with other material status symbols.

Saint Loup: Marcel visits him at Doncières which provides him with material for involuntary memory. The shadow of the cities of the plain looms over the handsome soldier, although this development in his character is scarcely perceptible yet. His character is to mutate later into one vaguely resembling that of the Baron de Charlus although his political attitudes on Dreyfusism are considerably more liberal on account of his military background which has drawn him away from the narrowness of aristocratic civilian life.

Rachel: The Jewish actress precipitates a love-jealousy syndrome in Saint Loup and heaps heavy financial demands upon the wealthy gentleman as well. She embodies social flux and "déclassement," for she emerges from virtually the bottom of society to a place near the top. As a personality, she is unpredictable in her moods which seem to be in constant flux. Her temperament runs in extremes, reaching an extreme of cruelty in her treacherous scheme against another actress to drive her off the stage. In love, she oscillates from the heat of passion to glacial coldness.

The Baron De Charlus: As well as being portrayed in terms of the sinister designs of his vice, he is also portrayed as a man of unstable and violent temper. He can scald people into submissiveness with his interminable ravings and piles avowed contempt and anti-Semitic fury upon the Jews. As the Jews are exiles in one sense, he is equally as much, if not more, an exile in another.

The Swanns: Marcel comes to recognize Mme. Swann as the former "lady in pink." Her opinions on the Dreyfus Case are illogical and hypocritical for a Jew's wife, but these views have allowed her to advance socially to Mme. de Villeparisis' salon. M. Swann is ill at this point and is becoming more unwelcome as a guest in high places due to the political climate of the times.

M. De Norpois: The stuffy diplomat is portrayed as shrewdly circumventing the inquiries of Bloch concerning the Dreyfus Affair as he gives forth a volley of ever-shifting double talk. The indolent Bloch is quite fooled and appears satisfied with the answers.

Dr. Cottard: Even though he will later turn into a man resembling Professor E., the punner emerges as a brilliant diagnostician and, in fact, appears to be the only decent doctor amid the entourage of quacks and incompetents who swarm about Marcel's grandmother and Bergotte. Proust's attitudes on the medical profession are directly and incisively presented.

Jupien: The little tailor is picked up from his brief early appearance in *Du Côté de chez Swann (Swann's Way)* and is generously described as a kindly person here. This sets him up for his horrifying appearance in the next novel.

IMAGERY IN LE CÔTÉ DE GUERMANTES (THE GUERMANTES WAY)

There is a sharp decline in the richness of Proust's **imagery** in this and immediately succeeding novels, for instead of presenting subjective poetic worlds, it focuses on the objective realities of society. Rather than dealing with Marcel's "invisible vocation" as its major **theme**, it deals with worldly elements a la "memoirs of Saint-Simon." There are, however, some images carried through from previous material such as the kaleidoscope image associated with the mutations of society, and the marine **imagery** associated with Albertine.

MOMENTS OF HEIGHTENED CONSCIOUSNESS IN LE CÔTÉ DE GUERMANTES (THE GUERMANTES WAY)

There is a compound memory sequence which Marcel experiences upon descending a staircase with Robert de Saint Loup in Paris, in which he experiences direct sensations of light, color, and weather conditions associated with Doncières, Combray, and Rivebelle. This recollection of better times past is anticipatory of the void through which he must pass before discovering firsthand his artistic commitment to writing.

The gurgling noise made by a steam radiator recently installed in his bedroom brings Marcel to think of Doncières and Balbec, and that sound is to always be intertwined in memory with the barracks town of Saint Loup. It recurs, also, in connection with Albertine's kiss in *The Sweet Cheat Gone*.

There is a sudden moment of happiness amid boredom and melancholy after the dinner at the Duc and Duchesse de Guermantes' house. The initial exhilaration of an incipient involuntary memory experience, however, quickly subsides and completely disappears.

SODOME ET GOMORRHE (CITIES OF THE PLAIN): PUBLISHING HISTORY AND GENERAL INTRODUCTION

This work, published in 1921 and 1922, was originally written in three volumes. It becomes readily noticeable that the author has become progressively more analytical and expository in his writing, this work opening with an analytical section which at the time of publication caused a public sensation.

SODOME ET GOMORRHE (CITIES OF THE PLAIN) PLOT SUMMARY*

The Guermantes are presented as the heirs of the two Biblical cities, their secret lives being depicted with both horror and compassion. We have the first meeting between the Baron de Charlus and Jupien. Marcel is finally invited to the Princesse de Guermantes' reception. Robert de Saint Loup alludes to a notorious servant of a Mme. de Potbus, a character figuring in Marcel's jealous suspicions over Albertine in later volumes. Marcel meets de Charlus again at the Princesse's gathering and now recognizes his problem. Afterwards Albertine visits Marcel again as their relationship deepens. He realizes that he is in love with her on his second visit to Balbec and takes her to dinner at La Raspelière of the Verdurins but discovers in conversation that she has known Mlle. Vinteuil and her friend. On the train trip to Raspelière, he and Albertine meet de Charlus on a platform watching Morel on the other side. Morel and de Charlus form a major plot element, sec ondary only to that of Marcel and Albertine. Through Morel, de Charlus enters Mme. Verdurin's ascending salon where he later snubs her by not introducing her to the Guermantes. Marcel persuades his reluctant mother to invite Albertine to stay with them in their Paris apartment. This novel develops the **theme** of Marcel's jealousy over Albertine which figures prominently in his plan to marry her so that he may draw her away from any other friends. A conspicuous parallel between Marcel's love and Swann's becomes apparent.

---

* Plot summaries and quotations are given with the permission of Alfred A. Knopf, Inc., and Random House, Inc.

THEMATIC STRUCTURAL ELEMENTS IN SODOME ET GOMORRHE (CITIES OF THE PLAIN)

The thematology of *Sodome et Gomorrhe* is centered around the following thematic material: that relating to the tragic aspects of "déclassement" in the snob-infested, anti-Dreyfus world of "society," that relating to jealousy in love, and that concerning itself with Marcel's disillusionments. The material may be divided into smaller sub-groups, but the above-mentioned three basically cover the most significant aspects of Proust's least well-received novel of *À la Recherche du temps perdu (Remembrance of Things Past)*.

The **Theme** of "Déclassement": Many forces are silently and insidiously at work as the eroding away of the facade of social class elements goes into its advanced stages. The major social affair of the novel, the reception of the Princesse de Guermantes, has a strongly depressing atmosphere, and Proust relies largely upon **satire** in recounting it. It is, in fact, to escape from this oppressive atmosphere amid social competition that Marcel retreats to Balbec on a second trip there.

The role of the secret lives of the aristocrats is of prominent significance, for as the recognized hierarchies become more amorphous with the ascendancy of the monied bourgeoisie, hidden hierarchies emerge. Marcel presents his treatise on homosexuality at the beginning of the novel, presenting the haunted, exiled souls with compassion in circumspect, elusive, image-laden language. This contained and objective essay written by an innocent but enlightened young man, however, is followed by the one singular most horrifying incident of the entire cycle. Not only is the meeting of the Baron de Charlus and Jupien itself horrifying, but it brings into focus the heretofore unresolved mystery of Montjouvain. This double impact is significant to Proust's design of a spiritual-death center of his three-phrase cycle, for we now find the reason for the placement of the Montjouvain incident in the otherwise idyllic *Du Côté de chez Swann (Swann's Way)*. The Montjouvain motif will crystallize around Albertine as well, when she inadvertently and innocently mentions knowing Mlle. Vinteuil to Marcel. Thus the Montjouvain incident gives symmetry to the novel cycle and serves as a Dantesque anteroom to the hell of the fourth novel's nether depths. As Marcel had viewed the window scene in the first novel unobserved, he likewise views the meeting of de Charlus and Jupien unobserved, this time from beneath a staircase outside Marcel's family's apartment at the Hôtel de Guermantes overlooking the courtyard. Ambiguity of gender there is indicative of a more colossal ambiguity, that suggesting the impending chaos of civilization. Émile Zola even postulated in his work that the abandonment of sexual morality is the sign that civilization itself is soon to be abandoned - an idea linking Zola's and Proust's work back to the Old Testament itself. As death seemed so inevitable in *Le Côté de Guermantes (The Guermantes Way)*, social decay and ultimate chaos seem inevitable here - and the Guermantes seem to be singled out to bear the curse. The aristocracy has become literally impotent, being gradually penetrated by the new, energetic, and financially potent bourgeoisie. The vulgar Verdurins are hideously wealthy, now mid-way to their conquest of the Princesse de Guermantes' palace. Gilberte has now come into a monstrous fortune from a deceased uncle of Swann's. The two pathways that were at one time so mutually exclusive are in the process of intersecting and ultimately becoming one.

The role of the Dreyfus Case is preeminent in *Sodome et Gomorrhe (Cities of the Plain)* for at its main social event, the reception at the Princess de Guermantes', false rumor has it that Swann has been ejected from the premises. While this might be easy to believe amid the anti-Semitic climate of the times, it develops to the contrary that M. Swann has been in private with the Prince, and Swann's subsequent account of his audience covers a large portion of the novel. The Princesse had gained the reputation for being notoriously anti Semitic, and we are surprised at this seeming inconsistence in their characters. Swann is a gentle assimilated Jew, and his attitudes on the Dreyfus Affair are moderate compared to those of the unassimilated Bloch who listens each day to the blow-by-blow court testimony.

Theme of Love-Jealousy: This theme overlaps various social elements in the novel and involves the Baron de Charlus and Morel, Robert de Saint Loup and Rachel, and Marcel and Albertine. Of paramount significance is the extreme degree of Marcel's jealousy over Albertine which manifests itself mildly when Marcel is made to wait for her telephone call. We are reminded that the anxiety incurred by this wait is like that incurred by the wait for his mother's goodnight kiss at Combray so many years ago. Marcel has come to take Albertine for granted, and he assumes that she will appear for him after the Princesse's party. When she fails to come, however, an onrush of anxiety overtakes him as he waits in his lonely room. Albertine finally calls on the telephone to explain her delay, and once he is assured that she is coming, he comes again to take her for granted. In fact, he enters upon a self inquiry as to what it could be in Albertine that appeals to him. Not seeming inaccessible to him, she seems vulgar and contemptuously familiar to him. He finally reaches a point where her pursuit of him becomes a bore, and he decides to break off the relationship. It is only with the arousing of his insane jealousy that he decides to marry her, a plan not designed for love but arising from an insane, wrathful jealousy that gives him the desire to imprison her. At Raspelière, Marcel had suggested that he would some time inquire with Mme.

Verdurin about Vinteuil's music. To hide her ignorance and vulgar tastes, Albertine suddenly volunteers information which innocently divulges her acquaintance with Mlle. Vinteuil and her friend. This disclosure has the impact of a Classical recognition scene, and it sets Marcel into a frenzy of memories of Montjouvain. He feels strangely terrible shudders of retribution, overcome by a vague but morbid sensation that he let his grandmother die, and experiences an unbearable grief reminiscent of the night at Combray as he kisses Albertine. When Marcel's mother calls to him to look at a pretty sunrise, all the stricken Marcel can see is a terrifying sunset over Montjouvain.

Theme of Marcel's Disillusionments: At the beginning of *Sodome et Gomorrhe (Cities of the Plain)*, Marcel goes from an extreme of almost culpable innocence whereby he is oblivious to the most obvious corruption in the Baron de Charlus, to the opposite extreme of disillusionment whereby nearly everyone appears in some way suspect. This bespeaks the degree of shock experienced by the narrator, and it pervades throughout the fourth and fifth novels of the cycle. It is to escape from the clamorous society, with which he is so disillusioned, that he takes his second trip to Balbec; but he is only to experience disillusionment in a more direct and personal way here. Balbec becomes identified with Albertine, and their liaison is solidly molded during this devastating second stay. Marcel's love for Albertine is thoroughly Proustian - entirely subjective, imbued with fantasy, and never reciprocal. Marcel externalizes an ego-vision in the typical way (à la Bergson-à la Proust) to bring forth a self-projection of the beloved, injecting a construct of his own into another person whom he treats as a 'tabula rasa' with no individual identity. The sadly disillusioning result is that the other person's inevitable individuality and needs for freedom are never anticipated. Like Albertine, Balbec itself also becomes a disillusionment - it loses all of its seeming mystery evoked by its name and their love relationship to Marcel by the end of the second summer. One can recall a disillusionment pattern anticipated in an ominously autumnal Balbec as early in the cycle as *À l'Ombre des jeunes filles en fleurs (Within a Budding Grove)*.

Other **themes** touched upon in *Sodome et Gomorrhe* find themselves included in some fine but scattered passages on the persistent **themes** of time and memory, reference to the suffering composer M. Vinteuil, and a momentously beautiful involuntary memory sequence involving life and death of which a description follows after the next segment.

CHARACTERIZATION IN SODOME ET GOMORRHE (CITIES OF THE PLAIN): METHODS OF PORTRAYAL

Marcel: The narrator is now portrayed as a disillusioned, suspicious, and jealous young man who has aged considerably. He frequently dreams of his grandmother and seems to hunger subconsciously for the beauty of his idyllic childhood.

Marcel's Mother: On the second trip to Balbec one year following the grandmother's death, Marcel's mother is portrayed as taking on every detail of the grandmother's ways, evidently in an effort to preserve her by subconsciously becoming her. She carries her bag and muff, and even reads from Mme. de Sévigné whom she had formerly considered amusing.

Albertine: Marcel's girlfriend arouses fanatical jealousy, but is a very commonplace and ordinary girl. The shadow of vice is cast upon Albertine by Dr. Cottard at the Casino at Incarville, and by Marcel who has belatedly realized the horror of Montjouvain. Of primary significance is the fact that Marcel will become more her captive than Albertine his. She also brings out the relentless traditionalism of Françoise.

The Baron De Charlus: Proust portrays this pathetic creature largely through **satire** and extremely acid "pastiche." His scorn for the crude Verdurins is nullified by his ironic connection with their protege who keeps de Charlus inextricably drawn into their circle. Morel is even more vulgar and indelicate than those the Baron scorns.

The Prince And Princesse: Their portrayal is designed to illustrate the unpredictability of the human temperament. Reputedly anti-Dreyfus and anti-Semitic, they receive Swann kindly and as a special guest at their reception.

Dr. Cottard: He is portrayed as a brilliant diagnostician who is now more polished in social circles, but is emerging as a snob and is taking on the qualities of the formidable Professor E.

MOMENTS OF HEIGHTENED AWARENESS IN SODOME ET GOMORRHE (CITIES OF THE PLAIN)

Despite the fact that many critics consider this novel to be the worst of the entire cycle, its "Intermittences of the Heart" sequence is one of the singular masterpieces of the work. It is an involuntary memory sequence and, consistent with this phase of the cycle, it is the one incident of this sort which exudes a tone of deep sadness. However, it carries the full exuberance of Proust's strange genius. Marcel, in his room at the Balbec Hôtel, reaches down to unbutton his boots and realizes at once that the actual presence of his grandmother is there from the trip before to assist him. The passage is masterful: it is not maudlin, but a lamentation of the first order, striking in its finality. Marcel's beloved grandmother, a mother-substitute on that first trip to Balbec, had at that time come to help him unbutton his boots as he entered exhausted - and now he realizes in a direct and devastatingly sad experience that she is gone. A transcendent presence fills that same room that he had occupied before, and he realizes suddenly that it is that of his grandmother. Since her death, nothing of her presence seemed to remain. But when Marcel's intuition discovers her presence, he at once realizes that it is irrevocably lost. This discovery of her intact presence is tormenting in its elusive beauty for a paradox of life preservation and death finality plays upon his mind - a hugely penetrating, authentic, and existential experience.

LA PRISONNIÈRE (THE CAPTIVE): PUBLISHING HISTORY AND GENERAL INTRODUCTION

La Prisonnière was published in 1923, the first novel of *À La Recherche du temps perdu* to be published after the author's death in 1922. Its content concerning Bergotte reveals Proust's consciousness of what was inevitably to come to him early in life. It also contains large blocks of expository material, typical of the central-and latter novels which are distinguished from the early ones in which the poetical rhythms and images are more animated.

PLOT SUMMARY OF LA PRISONNIÈRE (THE CAPTIVE)*

This novel penetrates further into the obsessive jealousy that Marcel harbors for Albertine and into all of his schemes to

---

* Plot summaries and quotations are given with the permission of Alfred A. Knopf, Inc., and Random House, Inc.

bind her as she in turn schemes to elude his possessiveness. She goes on mysterious sojourns with her friend Andree, and Marcel becomes ill to the point where he cannot leave the house. He finally locks her in the apartment. We have the brilliant passages of Marcel's description of Bergotte's death where we find the first **exposition** of his theories of life, death, Time and Eternity. The Morel-de Charlus plot continues with the Baron collaborating with Mme. Verdurin to give a musicale to present Morel's talents, a dazzling occasion at which he upstages her by refusing to introduce the bourgeois hostess to his aristocratic Guermantes circle. She takes her revenge by telling the ambitious young Morel that de Charlus is wanted by the police. Fearing exposure himself, Morel publicly denounces de Charlus who subsequently becomes ill. Marcel continues to keep Albertine captive in his apartment, but it is he who is more the captive than she. Françoise disapproves of Albertine, and the house is filled with suspicion and jealousy to which Marcel becomes passive. Eventually he decides that she bores him and considers traveling to Venice. On the morning he has resolved to go, he rings for Françoise and she tells him of Albertine's escape. She had left at nine that morning and left a letter for Marcel. Marcel is forlorn but, in a way, relieved.

THEMATIC STRUCTURAL ELEMENTS OF LA PRISONNIÈRE (THE CAPTIVE)

The most significant thematic material in *La Prisonnière* is that concerned with Marcel's jealousy for Albertine, Bergotte's contemplation of Vermeer's art, Marcel's reflections on Vinteuil's septet, and the final domination of the Baron de Charlus by Mme. Verdurin. The actual plot line of *La Prisonnière* is quite thin, and the novel takes on a renewed contemplative quality which lifts it from the depths of the previous two novels. Nevertheless, the de

Charlus-Morel subplot is elaborately constructed and shrewdly resolved. One may note, too, that *La Prisonnière (The Captive)* and the following *Albertine Disparue (The Sweet Cheat Gone)* are basically sequels, the latter finally resolving the drawn out Marcel-Albertine plot.

Theme of Jealousy: One could almost exclude the love element at this point from the Marcel-Albertine plot, for his motives in his planned marriage to her are simply for jealous purposes of domination. To some, the ensuing sequence of events surrounding her captivity seems overdrawn and lacking in probability, but it actually does bear similarity to real life cases even though some of the externalized story seems preposterous. Milton Hindus is among those who consider the plot material somewhat on the improbable side, but it is nevertheless sadly true as to the measures some people will take to simply dominate others - even when the illusion of lore has long since passed. In Marcel's case, the thought of someone he had idealized so fantastically and loved so unrealistically coming into her own and gaining other friendships is too much for him. This gives credibility, also, to his believing her to be corrupt on such flimsy evidence - her merely stating that she had been on friendly, sisterlike terms with Mlle. Vinteuil. Marcel must take out his wrath and shock, which came to him with overwhelming double strength in the previous novel, on Albertine. And so the once-beloved becomes a scapegoat for all the vice and evil of the world in general. Strangely, however, when Albertine finally escapes, Marcel's fury seems to have run its course and he feels a relief at being free from her himself. As the captive **theme** came into the cycle during the magic-lantern sequence of *Du Côté de chez Swann (Swann's Way)* in which Golo's pursuit of Genevieve de Brabant was reflected in casts of light around

Marcel's window curtains, it recurs and begins resolution in *La Prisonnière (The Captive)* with Albertine's escape.

Theme of Art: One of Proust's finest passages is that in which the novelist Bergotte discovers perfection in Vermeer's art by a simple but fascinating interplay of color **metaphor**. The painting in concern is Johann (Jan) Vermeer's "View of Delft," with which familiarity is imperative for understanding and appreciation of this triumphant passage. Like Proust himself, Bergotte attends an art exhibition while seriously ill and comes to feel faint while viewing Vermeer's painting. The expanded consciousness of illness plus the spell of the magnificent painting bring Bergotte to a heightened awareness which is recounted by Marcel who, like Proust, anticipates death. The "View of Delft" is a seventeenth-century painting depicting Vermeer's native Delft, with its typically Dutch stone buildings and its little church in which he was baptized, as viewed along a skyline of breaking clouds with the water of the Rotterdam Canal in the foreground. Its primary subjects are the sky, the city, and the water - but its highlight is the reflection of the sun against some facade and rock surfaces in the lower right hand portion of the picture. The yellow patch referred to in Proust is the most outstanding of these subtle highlights which not only joins the water to the city and sky but also gives the picture a tremendous sense of harmony and balance. Bergotte then proceeds to reflect on life and art in terms of a pair of scales. This **imagery** enhances the lament of the transitoriness of life on the one hand, and yet exults the triumphant permanence of art on the other - a permanence which even defies the fact that Vermeer was himself forgotten and unacknowledged for more than a century, his great work being recognized but attributed to other artists. When Bergotte dies, there is also another superlative passage contemplating whether or not he actually is mortal or not, suggestive of the idea that artists are immortal and raising the question of immortality in general. Vermeer's technique, like Elstir's, is one utilizing a metaphorical vision of ambiguity whereupon the water, city, and sky are joined together in an Impressionistic vision through the play of sunlight. The role of changing weather conditions also contributes to the advanced, fluid quality of Vermeer's work - weather techniques being considered innovative two centuries later with the dawn of impressionistic art in France's nineteenth century.

There are several other fine passages relating to the arts in *La Prisonnière (The Captive)* besides that just described transpiring at The Hague. Many of the passages are critical or are **expositions** on the redemptive nature of art itself. The most absorbing, however, are those pertaining to M. Vinteuil's music of which a septet emerges in *La Prisonnière (The Captive)*. Compiled by Mlle. Vinteuil and her friend as an artistic exorcism on her deceased father's behalf, it is played for the first time by the violinist Morel at the musicale at Mme. Verdurin's house (Quai Conti). During this concert, Marcel is propelled into an involuntary memory sequence in which recollections of the earlier and less complex Vinteuil sonata with its same "little phrase" come to mind, along with a transcendent joy anticipating another truer life beyond this one.

Theme of "Déclassement": In *La Prisonnière (The Captive)*, this theme reaches a dramatic peak with Mme. Verdurin's final domination and destruction of the Baron de Charlus following the concert in her house. This is carried out through a horrendous scheme perpetrated by a provoked and furious Mme. Verdurin in which she deliberately sets the Baron de Charlus' protege upon him and precipitates an ugly public scene. Engineered by the bourgeois hostess, she is finally able to avenge his ridicule and scorn which was culminated by his not introducing her to the Guermantes.

CHARACTERIZATION IN LA PRISONNIÈRE (THE CAPTIVE): METHODS OF PORTRAYAL

Bergotte: The writer is portrayed as an obvious projection of Proust himself at the time near his death. Proust had had a similar experience at an art exhibition several years before the writing of this novel and was a devoted admirer of Vermeer's paintings. Bergotte is at the height of his artistic receptivity in *La Prisonnière* and comes to rank with the other artist figures of the novel. It is only too late that he discovers the metaphorical triumph of Vermeer's perfect finishing touch of yellow on a sunlit wall.

Robert De Saint Loup: We begin to discover the mutating Saint Loup in sides of his psychological make-up that had been only barely perceptible in the immediately preceding novels.

Gilberte: She embodies "déclassement" for she is accepted everywhere in society on account of her huge inheritance from an uncle of Swann. This places an interesting commentary on the impotent aristocracy that had formerly excluded her on account of her being the daughter of a Jew and the stigmatized Odette. The aristocracy is becoming as money-conscious as the bourgeoisie that it had so scorned. In *La Prisonnière*, we learn of the death of Charles Swann, Gilberte's father.

Morel: The protege of the Baron de Charlus, whom we have come to know as an unpleasant character personally, emerges in this novel as a brilliant musician. He turns against the Baron because he fears for his public reputation and his future career as a concert violinist.

The Baron De Charlus: He comes to embody the ultimate downfall of the decadent aristocracy, becoming now more of an exile himself than the Jews whom he had referred to as "foreigners" in *Le Côté de Guermantes*. The arrogantly proud aristocrat falls to the mercy of the rising middle class and becomes the pathetic prey of the venomous Mme. Verdurin. Morel, who disgraces him in public, is the son of Marcel's uncle's valet.

IMAGERY IN LA PRISONNIÈRE (THE CAPTIVE)

Although this novel is not as rich in **imagery** as the first two, it brings back recurrent images from *Du Côté de chez Swann (Swann's Way)* such as that of the magic lantern. As Marcel contemplates the beauties of Vinteuil's music, the recurring images of the Martinville steeples and the tea and madeleine of Combray come back to him. And as he laments the anxieties imposed upon him by Albertine's turn away from his kiss, he recalls his mother's goodnight kiss which he missed so many years ago at Combray.

MOMENTS OF HEIGHTENED AWARENESS IN LA PRISONNIÈRE (THE CAPTIVE)

Memories of Combray and Doncières come back to Marcel as the olfactory sensation precipitated by burning twigs in his bedroom fireplace takes him back to his happy days as a boy. Although this is not among the strongest of the involuntary memory sequences in Proust, it is an absorbing and pleasant reverie triggered by an immediate sense perception.

Marcel is carried into a musical reverie in which he recalls popular songs from the cafe concert repertoire when he experiences the direct sensations incurred by the onslaught of cold weather. This sudden feeling, bordering on a chill, triggers involuntary memory of the concert music that was seemingly forgotten.

The most memorable and transcendent of the involuntary memory sequences of *La Prisonnière (The Captive)* takes place at the home of Mme. Verdurin during the concert which the Baron de Charlus had arranged for Morel. It is during this musicale that M. Vinteuil's septet is played for the first time, and its elusive "little phrase" magically evokes involuntary memory of the sonata. Marcel feels himself transported to some strangely distant country, and his exhilarated presentiment of timelessness and eternal joy in the realm beyond the transitory precipitates a reflective passage on the nature of art and genius.

Near the end of *La Prisonnière (The Captive)* another olfactory sensation takes Marcel back to a direct experience involving resurrected memory of earlier times - the volatile odor of gasoline. Even though this sequence is not of the magnitude of the great artistic passages, it nevertheless depicts an experience of involuntary memory carrying Marcel back to trips to the country.

PUBLISHING HISTORY AND GENERAL INTRODUCTION ALBERTINE DIPARUE (THE SWEET CHEAT GONE):

This novel, the sixth of the cycle, was published in 1925. In Marcel Proust's original manuscripts, the novel's title was *La Fugitive* and this has been retained in the annotated critical edition of *À la Recherche du temps perdu* published by Editions Gallimard. Because much of the material of Proust published posthumously was fragmentary and often unedited, sometimes variant material, or an alternate title, may appear.

PLOT SUMMARY OF ALBERTINE DISPARUE (THE SWEET CHEAT GONE)*

Marcel reflects upon Albertine's departure and attempts to lure her back in a scheme in which Robert de Saint Loup is sent to Albertine's aunt, Mme. de Bontemps, with a 30,000-franc gift for M. de Bontemps' campaign costs. This money is supposedly from an undisclosed friend engaged to their adopted Albertine who will break off the engagement if she does not return. Saint Loup complies with Marcel but mentions his own marriage plans without disclosing the girl's name (Gilberte). Marcel contemplates arousing Albertine's jealousy by writing to her of his considering having Andree stay with him. He still loves Albertine, but when he sends a telegram imploring her to return, he receives a telegram from Mme. de Bontemps informing him of her death.

Marcel calls at the Guermantes, and much to his surprise, sees Gilberte in their midst. Odette has married the Count de Forcheville and Gilberte has not only been adopted into nobility but possesses a huge fortune. Marcel has made numerous discoveries about Albertine's private life and is now aloof from Gilberte.

Marcel and his mother go to Venice where he receives a telegram from Gilberte which, because of the telgrapher's misreading a barely legible signature, he thinks is from Albertine. Leaving Venice, Marcel reads in a letter that Saint Loup plans to marry Gilberte. After the marriage, she invites Marcel to Tansonville and discloses the unpleasant side of Saint Loup's private life. She still loves Marcel, but he does not love

---

* Plot summaries and quotations are given with the permission of Alfred A. Knopf, Inc., and Random House, Inc.

her. Marcel despairs in not being able to recapture Combray. His self and his memories seem lost.

THEMATIC STRUCTURAL ELEMENTS IN ALBERTINE DISPARUE (THE SWEET CHEAT GONE)

The amount of significant thematic material in *Albertine Disparue* drops off considerably from the previous novels due to its comparative shortness in actual length and its primary role as a transitional work. It is, basically, an anticlimactic sequel to *La Prisonnière*, largely devoted to Marcel's expository introspection analyzing all of the various phases of jealousy, separation, and oblivion. Albertine is already gone, and this sixth novel exudes a feeling of falling action serving to lead into the conclusion which follows in the resurrection phase of the cycle in *Le Temps retrouvé*. The most important thematic material in *Albertine Disparue*, structurally relating it to the cycle as a whole, includes a major segment on jealousy and its ramifications, the infiltration of the aristocracy by the bourgeoisie, and the elemental quality of flux and unpredictability in the human personality.

Jealousy: A large segment of the sixth novel of *A la Re cherche du temps perdu* concerns itself exhaustively with literally all the phases of jealousy which one may experience, including those which even the jealous person himself would least expect. In the example of Marcel, he at first deludes himself after Albertine's abrupt departure of his dominance over her in imagining that she is merely playing 'hard to get' in a new phase of the prolonged cat-and-mouse game. However, the fluid and chance nature of human response places Marcel in even a posthumous jealousy syndrome. To satisfy some strangely morbid, masochistic urge to confirm his worst suspicions of Albertine, he actually embarks on reconnaissance missions into her character and psychological make-up by making personal inquiries amongst her friends and acquaintances. So deep is his obsessive jealousy that he even suspects her of dubious activity when no conclusive evidence ever comes forth. Even the corrupt Andree denies that Albertine has committed any shameful acts. Inevitably, however, Marcel is to undergo the process of "intermittence" of which the ever-decreasing oscillations of heat and cooling will lead eventually to oblivion. Oblivion, or "oubli," is a primary Proustian **theme** - this process of seeming forgetting serving as the unconscious preparatory stage for involuntary memory. Likewise, forgetting plays a significant role in the eventual discovery of overlooked great art. Memory and forgetting, therefore, work inextricably together in Proustian thematology even though "oubli" is the obverse of memory. In the case of Albertine, Marcel eventually foresees the time when he will no longer suffer over her - just as his passion for Gilberte, emotion over his grandmother, and adoration for the Duchesse had subsided.

"Déclassement": The **themes** of impotence of the aristocracy and impregnation of its highest circles by the bourgeoisie supply major thematic elements in *Albertine Disparue (The Sweet Cheat Gone)* and are ultimately resolved to their full extent in *Le Temps retrouvé (The Past Recaptured)*. The persistent image of the kaleidoscope again appears in the sixth novel as we learn of the new heights reached by Gilberte, the receding of the Dreyfus issue into history, and the increasingly overt changes in de Charlus and Saint Loup. The final blow to what little now remains of traditional social stratification will be the outbreak of the war to end all wars - of which the devastation will shatter all that remains of the mores as well as the class structure of the "ancient régime." This turn away from the way of life that had survived even the French Revolution is anticipated in the "fin de siècle" milieu of *Albertine Disparue (The Sweet Cheat Gone)* but makes its complete turn in the total destruction of the aristocratic Merovingean descendants by not only time but by World War I in *Le Temps retrouvé (The Past Recaptured)*.

Bergsonian Flux: In *Albertine Disparue (The Sweet Cheat Gone)*, we are prepared for the radical changes in major characters which will come into the glaring light of wartime and post-war Paris in the finale of the seventh novel. This deliberate setting of a depressing mood and atmosphere in this novel and in the first half of the next is instrumental to the transfiguring and redemptive impact of the final involuntary memory sequences. The human personality, including Marcel's own, is subject to Bergsonian flux and unpredictable change. As time slips relentlessly by, all things fall under the effects of change -except what Marcel discovers in the heavily neo-Platonic ending of the cycle.

CHARACTERIZATION IN ALBERTINE DISPARUE (THE SWEET CHEAT GONE): METHODS OF PORTRAYAL

Marcel: This novel's portrayal of Marcel establishes him as despairing of his writing career as he reads the unfulfilling work of commercial journalists. He becomes conscious of the ravages of time to an almost irrevocable point as he visits Venice with his mother. It is in Venice, however, that he crosses the uneven flagstones in the baptistry of St. Mark's Cathedral, a magnificent example of Renaissance architecture. It was originally John Ruskin who inspired Marcel Proust to examine and write upon Venetian art and architecture.

Gilberte: She sadly emerges as Mlle. de Forcheville, having risen in the social milieu on account of her enormous inheritance from a Jewish relative. Ironically, however, she has tragically renounced her common background - for we discover that it would have pleased Swann to see his daughter's success.

Legrandin: Once a pretentious pseudo-literary social climber hilariously described in terms of his posterior in *Du Côté de chez Swann (Swann's Way)*, he is now disillusioned with the boring superficiality of high society.

Bloch: Formerly portrayed as the crude, unassimilated Jew who was a social outcast, he is now portrayed as an integral part of post-Dreyfus society but as also disenchanted by it.

Aimé: Introduced earlier in the cycle as the head waiter of the Grand Hôtel at Balbec, he now plays the sinister role of sleuth carrying out Marcel's prying orders to investigate Albertine's personal past.

MOMENTS OF HEIGHTENED AWARENESS IN ALBERTINE DISPARUE (THE SWEET CHEAT GONE)

Because Marcel spends nearly all of his time during the course of *Albertine Disparue* in the seclusion of his home, much as Proust was doing at the time the novel was written, his consciousness of outside weather conditions comes into significant play in heightening his contemplative sense of solitude and isolation. The particular instances of such weather phenomena involve themselves in involuntary memory although not of the magnitude of the tea-madeleine or boot-unbuttoning sequences. One involuntary memory sequence in *Albertine Dusparue* involves the effect of rainfall on Marcel, with its bringing forth lilac fragrances which trigger a succession of memories. In another, rays of sunlight outside Marcel's apartment on the balcony remind him of the Champs-Élysées. In yet another, the sound of the winds and the onset of Eastertide resurrect his yearnings for the past in historical Brittany and Venice. And yet again, the familiar sound of water gurgling in a steam radiator brings Marcel back to Albertine's kiss, just as the touch of a scarf reminds him of his former beloved.

LE TEMPS RETROUVÉ (THE PAST RECAPTURED): PUBLISHING HISTORY AND GENERAL INTRODUCTION

The final novel of *la Recherche du temps perdu (Remembrance of Things Past)* was published in 1927, and as has been mentioned before; much of the material in *Le Temps retrouvé (The Past Recaptured)* was written at the same time as *Du Côté de chez Swann (Swann's Way)* and is of the same high quality. The expository quality of the prose in this novel, however, sets it apart somewhat from the first of the cycle, but much of the **exposition** on art is superlative. Elstir's art is analyzed in a magnificent passage presenting it as representing the new technique of Impressionism, while Vinteuil's chamber composition is presented as representing the new music in another brilliant passage. And La Berma's embrace with Classicism and Bergotte's credos link the traditional with the modern. Of course, one must not overlook the capitalization of "Temps" in the title of the novel in which its attributes of Deity are discovered in its capacity for permanent preservation in art. This distinguishes the "Temps" of *Le Temps retrouvé* from the "temps" of *À la Recherche du temps perdu*. Much of the content of *Le Temps retrouvé* is jumbled for Proust died before he could revise it, but exhaustive efforts at restoring it in the chronological perspective of the other novels and the earlier-written finished fragments of *Le Temps retrouvé* have made recent editions more coherent to the reader. Likewise, C. K. Scott-Moncrieff died before he could translate this last novel or make any finished attempts at synthesizing its pieces into a whole. Nevertheless, the task has been undertaken by Frederick Blossom, Stephen Hudson, and most recently by Andreas Mayor.

PLOT SUMMARY OF LE TEMPS RETROUVÉ (THE PAST RECAPTURED)*

The final novel of the cycle recapitulates material from the others and sets down in final form Marcel's discovery of the "way" of art. Marcel visits Saint Loup at Tansonville where he recalls first observing Gilberte. Some years pass, Marcel is in a sanatarium, and the Great War begins. Marcel returns to Paris, finding it bleak and deserted. Saint Loup dies a war hero. The widowed Mme. Verdurin has a fortune, and the pathetic de Charlus is pro-German. The war ends, and Marcel is a semi-invalid who has lost interest in life - but he attends a musicale presented by the new Princesse (formerly Mme. Verdurin). On the way he encounters the invalid-mental case de Charlus attended by Jupien but repudiated by all classes of respectable society.

Entering the mansion, Marcel stumbles on an uneven flagstone, bringing back memories which are further enhanced within the library where he awaits the conclusion of a musical performance before entering the salon. He discovers more than memory, but a key suspending time and recapturing lost time.

In the salon, Marcel sadly discovers that time's irrevocable forces have changed all of the people whom he once thought he knew. The Duc has become the lover of the former Odette Swann (Mme. de Forcheville); the Duchesse has become friendly with Rachel. Finally Gilberte introduces Marcel to her daughter - embodying the final mingling of aristocratic and bourgeois lineage.

---

* Plot summaries and quotations are given with permission of Alfred A. Knopf, Inc., and Random House, Inc.

Retrieving lost time, Marcel begins his novel - to place recaptured Time in permanent artistic form.

THEMATIC STRUCTURAL ELEMENTS IN LE TEMPS RETROUVÉ (THE PAST RECAPTURED)

Thematically, this final novel of *À La Recherche du temps perdu* brings the disparate threads of the cycle into a final recapitulation and resolution. As we enter this seventh novel, the **theme** of Marcel's disillusionment has given way to complete disenchantment. He even sees no hope or edification in literature. Such writers as the Goncourts in their Journal impress him as shallow and commercial. Their quixotic vision of Mme. Verdurin's salon is aglitter with all of the phoniness and extravagance of wealth. The whole scene reminds us of what are referred to today in America as "the beautiful people," and is reminiscent to an American of one of the Paris traveler F. Scott Fitzgerald's ballroom scenes in the doomladen *The Great Gatsby*. By *Le Temps retrouvé*, many of the Proustian characters have mutated as souls are doomed in Eastern mysticism to the successive reincarnations in the vicious death-birth-death circle of samsara - a continual, never-ending bondage to the chains of time. Robert de Saint Loup and the Baron de Charlus have, in fact, progressed to something far more disastrous than samsara: they are living in a Dantesque hell in which their sins themselves have become their tormenting punishment. People, the world, and writing itself - all are in a downward spiral at the beginning of *Le Temps retrouvé*. This final novel brings the whole problem of man's condition and his identity into sharp focus. All seems destroyed by time, Marcel having come to experience this prominently in Venice during the final course of *Albertine Dusparue (The Sweet Cheat Gone)*. All elements of identity have seemed to collapse for Marcel: childhood, class lines, temporal delineations, love, friendship, society, writing. Upon Marcel's return to Tansonville in his final encounter with his former-beloved Gilberte, Combray now presents the spectre of a thoroughly dull, ugly little town. The magical Combray of Marcel's childhood identity seems irrevocably lost; and Gilberte, whom he at first does not even recognize, reminds him of a coarse, superficial painted woman he recalls glimpsing earlier in life. The sense of flux, change, and impermanence is overwhelming.

Theme of Proustian Love-Disillusionment: Even in *Le Temps retrouvé (The Past Recaptured)*, the basic pattern endures, applying now to Gilberte's relationship with Saint Loup. Marriage in the Guermantes circle has degenerated to a mere financial expediency as the aristocratic Robert de Saint Loup has married the rich Gilberte for her fortune, and likewise, as the Prince de Guermantes has married his newbourgeois wife for her wealth after the death of Oriane. Despite the cold calculations of monetary concerns amid marital matters, Gilberte is ensnarled in a jealousy syndrome with Robert. It develops that she has become infuriated over his consorting with other women - but, more significantly paramount to his character, it develops as to why he has so unabashedly pursued women. Gilberte experiences a possessive jealousy toward Saint Loup similar to that experienced by Marcel for her years earlier. It is now Saint Loup and Marcel who are cool toward Gilberte.

Marcel's Invisible Vocation: The purpose for the inclusion of the passage from the Goncourt Journal is twofold. One is to present Marcel with the most superficial, discouraging, and utterly meaningless piece of writing possible so that we may be given just cause for his disenchantment with literature. The other is to show a journalist's objective vision of the Verdurins, who have acquired certain elements of finesse and cultivation by this time after considerable exposure to aristocracy and leisure pursuits. The main point of Proust's presenting the journalists' vision of the Verdurins, however, is to demonstrate the subjective Bergsonian element of what is seen through different people's eyes. The journalists' "beautiful" people are often the acquainted individual's boors.

Theme of Social Comment (the "memoirs" of Saint-Simon of another period): Of patent significance to this **theme** is that we are told outright that the Méséglise Way and the Guermantes Way are no longer irreconcilable. We find ourselves eventually in the throes of the Great War with Paris going up in flames both literally and spiritually, as the two cities in Genesis fell to Jehovah's wrath by fire. Swann's last premonitory dream involved a vision of Odette amid a city afire, also. Later, we find ourselves in a sterile post-war Paris, the material about wartime Paris being an insertion placed into the work during that time. Its effect, along with the references to Marcel's two stays in sanitariums, is one of stretching the novel's ending away from the Tansonville encounter with Gilberte and to extend the period of disillusionment.

Marcel Proust utilizes the techniques of the Russian writers in his lamenting the passing of the old order (in his case, the lifestyle of the "ancien régime"), and of the classical memoirists in his satirical pastiches of the Goncourts and of the empty husks of characters. Dreyfusism, the polarizer of France at the "fin de siècle," has now shrunk away into oblivion as a non-issue - being superseded by World War I. Mme. Verdurin has capitalized on the war, using her contacts with politicians to escalate her social ascendancy. The Jews prove themselves as patriots even though men like Bloch remind us a little of Philip Roth's Sheldon Grossbart in "Defender of the Faith." And despite the fact that we know of Saint Loup's descent from Sodom and of his kinship therefrom to de Charlus, we are still confirmed of his valor in battle. Upon looking back, however, to *A l'Ombre des jeunes filles eneurs (within a Budding Grove)*, we realize how little idea Saint Loup had of the prolonged time the war would take. His naive notions of military efficiency give him to believe that peace will be accelerated by the terror of modern weaponry. Marcel himself at the end quietly abhors the useless and bloody war. Despite the holocaust, Mme. Verdurin's ascent and M. de Charlus' descent progress as usual as Marcel again observes the Baron engaged in his now-overt private eccentricity.

A major sector of *Le Temps retrouvé (The Past Recaptured)* deals with Marcel's emergence from seclusion and his acceptance of the invitation to the matinee at the Prince de Guermantes' mansion. Sadly, Marcel accepts the invitation to the Guermantes rather than the conflicting one to a party given by La Berma. The once great actress has now been superseded by Rachel and is now a solitary being whose kin even go to the Guermantes'. Little does Marcel know, however, that the Princesse de Guermantes who invited Marcel is not the Princesse he has known but quite another - a mutated Mme. Verdurin whom the widowed Prince has married for her money. Marcel's old friends and acquaintances are scarcely recognizable, as Gilberte and Combray became scarcely recognizable. What we see at the matinee of those characters that Marcel and the reader thought they knew is evidence of their change. Everyone has aged. The once-esteemed Duchesse associates with Rachel and other entertainers - formerly a social taboo. And Bloch has penetrated the Guermantes circle.

Themes of Memory, Time, and Art: There are six tremendously prominent involuntary memory sequences in *Le Temps retrouvé (The Past Recaptured)*, bringing the total of heightened awareness moments in the cycle to twenty-two. Five of the six occurring in *Le Temps retrouvé*, however, are interlocked and are frequently treated as one multi-moment. Details of these moments themselves will appear in the separate segment on moments of heightened awareness, but one could take note in passing of their Platonic quality. Like the liberated captives from the allegorical cave in *The Republic*, Marcel seems suddenly stunned as the captives were momentarily blinded by the light of Truth and Essential Reality from the sun after becoming habituated to the delusion of shadows moving against a wall. The student with a basic understanding of Plato's *Doctrine of Forms* (or *Essences*) and his *Doctrine of Reminiscences* will come to appreciate Marcel's ascent from depression upon apprehending eternal Truth in art. The Proustian contribution to this neo-Platonism is an extension of the concept of Truth lying in the unconscious, and its being tapped by the process of involuntary memory.

The material in *Le Temps retrouvé (The Past Recaptured)* about the war and social change serves mainly to give us a backdrop for Marcel's discovery of that Reality which has remained intact. This will constitute Proust's theory of art which underlies the entire *À la Recherche du temps perdu* cycle. The narrator outlines his whole synthesized aesthetic of creative Truth which encompasses his direct interdisciplinary experience with Vinteuil, Elstir, Bergotte, and La Berma. The novel cycle becomes an analysis of Proust's own method, presented through Marcel's vision of the place of art in life. This serves as the foundation for Marcel's resolved literary career. It is here that Time is cast into the permanence of art through the temporal **metaphor** of involuntary memory, thus the capitalization of "Temps." The novel ends with the word "time" completing the thematic circle from its induction at the beginning of *Du Côté de chez Swann (Swann's Way)*.

Marcel realizes that the past, gone though it may seem to be, can not only be recovered by memory, but its inner reality can be preserved by art. This conviction of the permanence, coupled with man's longing for immortality, propels Marcel to devote his final years to writing a book - a great work of art which will accomplish the end of preserving life. In the cycle of novels, there have been three "ways" -two with which we have been familiar from the beginning (the Méséglise Way, the "way" of passion and love; and the Guermantes Way, the "way" of the world and society) and a third - the "way" of art. This intimacy with art has been subtly growing throughout *À la Recherche du temps perdu* - creativity residing in Vinteuil, Elstir, Bergotte, and La Berma. Despite the fact that everyone at the Princesse's matinee seems grotesquely transmogrified, Elstir's art is analyzed in a superlative passage and it stands for the new technique of Impressionism; Vinteuil's chamber composition represents a new music; and yet La Berma's classicism and Bergotte's credos link and resolve the traditional with the modern. Art is able to stem a relentless flow of time and transfigures suffering into Beauty. Vinteuil, out of suffering, created immortal music, providing the otherwise worldly existences of Swann and Marcel with what the existentialists call the "authentic" - emerging from the Absurd. Art, like religion, has the power to heal: it provides us with our conquest over time and over death.

CHARACTERIZATION IN LE TEMPS RETROUVÉ (THE PAST RECAPTURED): METHODS OF PORTRAYAL

Marcel: The narrator is portrayed in a resurrection, resolving and finally eclipsing the death phase of the full cycle. Nevertheless, Marcel's protracted book is a riddle to the reader, for the reader is left with the enigmatic question of whether the book we have just read is Marcel's writing retrospectively from his point of self-recognition at the Princesse's mansion - or whether it is a yet-to-be written book which we are to fathom in our minds as a synthesis of the firsthand experiences we have shared with the first-person narrator.

Gilberte: For artistic unity, we see her once again at Tansonville where we originally caught our first enchanted glimpses of the daughter of Swann. She is now, by contrast, hardened and embittered by her marriage and fortune. Symbolically, she has a sixteen year-old daughter who enhances the cyclical formation of the cycle and of life.

The Baron De Charlus: The fallen aristocrat has struck the depths of degradation, having plummeted to the depths of a Dantesque hell. The vision we have of his sin is that it has now reached a point where it has become its own punishment, bereft of any satisfactions that it might have at one time mysteriously afforded. The punishments of de Charlus are in the hell which he has himself created, and they emerge in an eternal rather than temporal light.

The Duc: He appears in *Le Temps retrouvé (The Past Recaptured)*, as a pathetic mutation of the arrogant man we once knew in *Le Côté de Guermantes (The Guermantes Way)*. He is pursuing Odette now and arouses our pity despite his crassness in matters of life and death earlier in the work.

Bloch: The formerly shunned Jew has penetrated the Guermantes circle, pointing out the kaleidoscopic changes social structure undergoes with the passing of a few years. One can notice similar shifts in U. S. public opinion, in controversial matters as well, as time passes.

La Berma: We learn of her decline and death in *Le Temps retrouvé (The Past Recaptured)*. She has been upstaged and eclipsed by the aggressive Rachel.

In concluding this final segment on the characters, one might take a brief look at the pyramid of characters in the book in terms of the three generations which overlap within the approximate forty-year span of *À la Recherche du temps perdu*. Included in the oldest generation of characters are Marcel's grandmother, her former schoolmate Mme. de Villeparisis, and the latter's consort M. de Norpois. The middle generation is that of the narrator's parents, which includes M. Charles Swann, Odette de Crecy, the Duc and Duchesse de Guermantes, the Baron de Charlus, the Verdurins, and Françoise. The narrator's own generation includes his schoolfriend Bloch, Gilberte, Albertine, Robert de Saint Loup, Morel, and Mlle. Vinteuil. From this point, it is a simple matter to deduce the generation of the other characters.

MOMENTS OF HEIGHTENED AWARENESS IN LE TEMPS RETROUVÉ (THE PAST RECAPTURED)

If one wishes to include the moment of incipient involuntary memory prior to the arrival at the Guermantes' mansion, when Marcel finds himself suddenly in a train that has stopped in the open country, then one would count seven moments of heightened awareness in *Le Temps retrouvé*. Marcel feels the vibrations of incipient memory, but the experience is absorbed by his overriding frame of mind and the vagueness of the sensation. This experience in the train is anticipated by and similar to that after the dinner at the Duc de Guermantes' in *Le Côté de Guermantes (The Guermantes Way)*.

Of the experiences of pure involuntary memory, however, the first in this final novel finds Marcel walking along the poorly paved streets in the vicinity of the mansion at which time he recalls days gone by when he walked along the Champs-Élysées with the governess Françoise. The sensation underfoot of rough road surfacing triggers the memory, which in turn anticipates the following involuntary memory sequence in the courtyard of the Guermantes' mansion.

The five succeeding experiences of involuntary memory, beginning with the courtyard flagstone sequence resurrecting the immediacy of St. Mark's baptistry in Venice, are frequently treated as one large multiple involuntary memory occurrence due to the fact that it seems to work in chain reaction, each experience being related to and dependent upon the others. During the trip with his mother, Venice seemed dull and oppressive due largely to the fact that the trip's purpose was one of escape from the memory of Albertine. Later, however, the essence of Venice is unexpectedly trapped in that second when Marcel stubs his toe on an uneven flagstone - an experience analogous to his stumbling in St. Mark's. The majesty of the Renaissance architecture that John Ruskin loved so well comes to Marcel with uncontaminated purity. The recaptured past holds that metaphorical secret of permanence that the past itself at the time did not hold. It is from this state of expanded consciousness that the four succeeding precious moments come forth.

Presently, as Marcel enters the mansion and is shown to the library to await the conclusion of a portion of the concert, he is reminded of Balbec by a sound reminding him of the local small-gauge train's brakeman tapping wheels to test the brakes. The railwayman's hammer is resurrected by the accidental striking of a spoon against a plate by one of the servants. Both experiences are relatively commonplace, but their metaphorical tie by their analogous sensations and disparity in time give them a new and magical dimension. The total effect of **metaphor** is mysteriously more than the sum of the parts. An ordinary row of trees is now enlivened.

The following experiences are metaphorically interesting as well, particularly that involving a cross-correspondence between the tactile sense and the visual. As Marcel experiences an inter-sense response in his memory of the Balbec train in reliving the olfactory sensation of burning wood, he likewise experiences an inter-sense response upon bringing a starched napkin to his brow. Upon observing its color, he is taken back to the marine blue of Balbec. The now familiar sound of steam gurgling through heating pipes again calls Marcel forth to Balbec as it had earlier in *Albertine Disparue (The Sweet Cheat Gone)*. Finally, the present is securely locked to the treasure of the early days in Combray by the one final piece in the huge puzzle that suddenly makes the whole picture of his future plans complete. In the process of artistic transfiguration in his discovery of time metaphor and the author's creative task in preserving it, he is enlivened in his resolve to dedicate his life to writing upon seeing a volume of George Sand's pastoral novel, François le Champi, on the library shelf. Amid the strains of Vinteuil's "ultra-violet" phrase alluded to in *Du Côté de chez Swann (Swann's Way)*, Marcel's eye is caught by the red binding on the book which his mother had read to him on that fateful night in Combray which was so crucial in the formation of Marcel's hypersensitive artistic temperament. Despite his despondency over literature, he now turns back to it.

The unfolding of the involuntary memory material in *Le Temps retrouvé (The Past Recaptured)* is in typical Proustian fashion. Marcel is in low spirits: driving to the matinee, he finds the world purposeless. Upon seeing those whom he once thought he knew, he finds the world absurd, endowed profusely with a quality referred to frequently in Proust - "néant," or "nothingness." As the afternoon progresses, however, he has both the mystical experience and the meditation upon it. Following the succession of involuntary memory experiences, expository passages of a superior order present the construct and technique of Proustian art. Material from that section will appear in the segment on Proust's style.

REMEMBRANCE OF THINGS PAST

THREE CIRCLES OF CHARACTERS

The three basic groups of characters in the novel cycle include the following: (1) those of the bourgeois circle of Marcel the narrator, which include his family and friends; (2) those of the new-bourgeois circle of the assimilated Jewish stockbroker's son, Swann, which include his family and their social contacts; and (3) those of the aristocratic Guermantes circle, which include their peers of the exclusive Faubourg Saint-Germain and their underlings. There are four basic classes of characters in the novel cycle: the crumbling aristocracy, the rising bourgeoisie, the Jews, and the servants.

THE CIRCLE OF MARCEL

Marcel: the narrator of the novel cycle whose reactions to social stratification, loves, and aspirations to become a writer form the preeminent **themes** of the novel cycle. His childhood is identified with his family and Combray; his growth and disillusionments with Gilberte, Albertine, and Saint Loup are identified with the non-reality of love and friendship in Balbec,

Paris, and Doncières; and his maturity is identified with his discoveries of art, timelessness, and his resolve to at last write. The entire narration of *À la Recherche du temps perdu (Remembrance of Things Past)* is the projection that we have the privilege to share firsthand of what Marcel ultimately will write in his own novel.

Marcel's Mother: the mother of the narrator who is remembered for her staying with him all night when as a child he had missed his goodnight kiss. She is connected with the sustained references to George Sand's (Lucile-Aurore Dupin's) François le Champi which she read to him that night. She is cultivated and gentle and is of crucial importance in the development of a frail and self-indulgent personality in Marcel. She takes on the grandmother's ways after her death, and she accompanies Marcel on a trip to Venice in *Albertine Disparue (The Sweet Cheat Gone)*. She is not a social climber and, like the rest of Marcel's people, is a liberal in the Captain Dreyfus Affair.

Marcel's Grandmother: the beloved grandmother of the narrator has a significant presence in the first three novels of the cycle, and several incidents prefigure her death which is to come by a stroke suffered in the Champs-Élysées in *Le Côté de Guermantes (The Guermantes Way)*. The premonitory and retrospective sequences concerning the death of the grandmother will be commented upon in the separate studies of the novels. The grandmother had attended convent school with the semi-aristocratic Mme. de Villeparisis, and by renewing the friendship, serves as an important link between Marcel and such figures of the Faubourg Saint-Germain as the Duchesse de Guermantes and Robert de Saint Loup. She enjoys reading the memoirs of de Sévigné and frequently quotes from the repertoire of seventeenth-century Classicists.

Uncle Adolphe: the subject of an early recollection of Marcel in which a "lady in pink" was observed present in his room. After the childlike Marcel inadvertently tells of Adolphe's visitor, the errant uncle is forthwith banished from the household. The memory of his room is evoked in *À l'Ombre des jeunes filles en fleurs (Within a Budding Grove)* by the mouldy smell resembling orris root in a Champs-Élysées pavilion.

Aunt Léonie: Marcel's hypochrondriacal, bedridden aunt (the widowed Mme. Octave) who owns the country estate at Combray around which his childhood memories revolve. She is the daughter of a cousin of Marcel's maternal grandmother, is vividly described in a small number of strokes, and is remembered by Marcel for giving him tea and madeleine on a Sunday morning before Mass when he was a small boy. We learn of Aunt Léonie's death in *À l'Ombre des jeunes filles en fleurs (Within a Budding Grove)*.

Françoise: the impeccably loyal cook and housekeeper of Marcel's family. One of the most fully drawn and individualized characters of the entire work, she appears throughout the cycle to emerge eventually as almost the master, rather than the servant, of Marcel in *La Prisonnière (The Captive)*. She is fierce and unrelenting in her traditionalism and in her performance of duties, having her cruel side as well as her humorous qualities.

M. Vinteuil: a neighbor of Marcel's family, appearing first as an insignificant piano teacher, but emerging posthumously as a recognized master of composition. His brilliant seven-note "little phrase" motif is intertwined with all of the major **themes** of the novel cycle: love, jealousy, memory, time, eternity. Vinteuil is a tragic figure, for his genius is born of mingled love and suffering caused by his psychologically sick daughter.

Mlle. Vinteuil: the composer's mentally ill daughter whom Marcel unintentionally views unobserved through a window at Montjouvain, and who figures in the loss of Marcel's idealized childhood vision of Combray and in his presentiments concerning people's hidden lives in the Faubourg Saint-Germain. She has tormented her father but also given rise to his highest creative accomplishments through his love for her.

M. Legrandin: a bourgeois engineer who considers himself a poet and enjoys using high flown, bookish language. His primary significance lies in the uncovering of his vice of "snobisme," and his comic portrayal suggestive of a secret life.

Albert Bloch: an unassimilated Jewish schoolfriend of Marcel's whose family includes his father, sisters and an uncle. He gives negative impressions of clumsy ill-manneredness, tactless vulgarity, and awkward intellectualism to Marcel's family. His views on poetry evolve from his early espousal of the obscure poets, but his self-consciousness is manifest throughout in his forced intellectualism and cruel snobbery. Bloch is excluded from Marcel's house when the narrator discloses the fact that Bloch has been circulating a rumor concerning one of his aunts. Bloch figures significantly in the novel, however, for he lends Marcel a book by Bergotte who will become his favorite living writer.

M. De Norpois: a former old-order diplomat and friend of Marcel's father. He is a pompous snob who feigns intellectualism in the arts. He has encouraged Marcel to see La Berma in a performance of the Classical "Phaedra," but he upbraids the "Art for Art's Sake" school in general and Bergotte in particular at the matinee of Mme. de Villeparisis at the beginning of *À l'Ombre des jeunes filles en fleurs (Within a Budding Grove)*. Marcel's grandmother has avoided intimacy with her old schoolmate, Mme. de Villeparisis, on account of the social taboo of her having been the mistress of M. de Norpois.

Albertine: She appears first as one of a group of young girls at Balbec, becoming identified with the Norman seaside resort in Marcel's eyes. She is an orphan reared somewhat grudgingly by an aunt, Mme. de Bontemps, who seems eager to get rid of her. She has no social status, but takes a peculiar pride in the fact that her name is spelled "Simonet" with only one "t." The obsessively jealous and disillusioning relationship between Marcel and Albertine is anticipated and set up during Marcel's first stay at Balbec; complicated by liaisons in Paris; and molded solidly during the second stay at Balbec; and brought to a head by her captivity in Paris. Albertine's death by a fall from a horse is reported in a telegram.

Elstir: one of the most important artist figures in the work. He is first introduced as the submissive Master Biche of the aggressive Mme. Verdurin's salon, but emerges as a fabulously brilliant and aesthetically mature artist with his discovery of misty Balbec seascapes. He becomes a master of impressionistic ambiguity whose vision of perception is based on "metaphor." We are reminded of Claude Monet and Gustave Morand when we consider Elstir's style visually. Marcel is enthralled by his work and meets him through Gilberte Swann.

La Berma: one of the prominent artist figures in the novel, she is a great actress in portraying Classical heroines like Racine's queen in "Phaedra." She represents Marcel's first contact with the formal arts and seems to be modeled after the French actress, Sarah Bernhardt.

THE SWANN CIRCLE

Charles Swann: the wealthy assimilated Jewish stockbroker's son who figures prominently in Marcel's memories of Combray, especially of the night his mother neglected to kiss him good night. "Un Amour de Swann" is his story relating his love affair with Odette de Crecy, which is pieced together from family conversations and village talk. There is at least an indirect link between Swann and nearly every other character in the cycle. We last see him at the conclusion of *Le Côté de Guermantes (The Guermantes Way)* and he is subsequently written out of the story with our hearing only indirectly of his death.

Odette De Crecy: There is no clue at first that Uncle Adolphe's "lady in pink" is Odette, but we discover that she is one of the mutating characters in the cycle. She emerges as Elstir's "Miss Scaripant," becomes the mistress and wife of Swann, becomes Mme. de Forcheville after Swann's death, and eventually is the attraction of the Duc de Guermantes. She figures most prominently in *Du Côté de chez Swann (Swann's Way)* as Swann's lover from the Verdurins' salon who arouses his obsessive jealousy.

Gilberte Swann: the daughter of Swann and Odette who becomes the childhood attraction of Marcel who recalls seeing her in the Champs-Élysées and through the hawthorn hedge at Tansonville. Even though Gilberte's name is barely legitimized by Swann's marriage to Odette, she is to eventually penetrate the heretofore impregnable Faubourg Saint-Germain. Marcel is first attracted to Gilberte because she represents a forbidden world to him, but becomes more drawn to her as he observes her being taken sightseeing by Bergotte. When Odette marries de Forcheville, Gilberte gains a noble name through adoption and inherits a fortune through a Swann relative. She eventually marries Robert de Saint Loup for his money. She gradually changes from being Marcel's idealized vision of a young girl to become a coldly pragmatic social climber.

Bergotte: Marcel's favorite living novelist whose aesthetic vision is embodied in his unique approach to **imagery** which gives his prose a transcendent musical quality. He is an "art for art's sake" writer whom M. de Norpois detests, but Bergotte's **imagery** has for Marcel the power of revelation. The sequence describing his death in *La Prisonnière (The Captive)* gives us a capsule of his vision of life, death, time, and eternity - as he views Vermeer's spellbinding and yet seemingly commonplace "View of Delft."

Mme. Verdurin: the despotic nouveau riche Parisian who professes a "snobisme" toward what she considers to be an idle aristocracy of "bores," but who herself ascends to its sacrosanct pinnacle in her third marriage by which she becomes the Princesse de Guermantes when the Prince marries her for her money. Mme. Verdurin's bourgeois salon figures prominently in *Du Côté de chez Swann (Swann's Way)* as the setting for the original playing of the unknown M. Vinteuil's enchanting "little phrase" and Swann's meeting Odette. Mme. Verdurin, despite her denigrations of social superiors, is infuriated at the Baron de Charlus' refusal to introduce her to the Guermantes at Morel's opening. Among the other characters who emerge from her salon are Vinteuil, Elstir, Bergotte, Brichot, "Ski," and Dr. Cottard.

Brichot: a Professor at the Sorbonne, of Mme. Verdurin's "clan," who is intellectual in historical and philosophical subjects, but who is not particularly adroit socially.

Dr. Cottard: a Professor of the Faculty of Medicine, one of Mme. Verdurin's "clan," whose bad puns and social crudity are surpassed only by his clinical excellence and scientific sophistication. He appears at first as a fool in *Du Côté de chez Swan (Swann's Way)* but has ascended to renown before *À l'Ombre des jeunes filles en fleurs (Within a Budding Grove)* ends.

"Ski": a Polish sculptor whose full name is Viradobetski. He is a minor artist figure in the work.

Count De Forcheville: Odette Swann's lover and husband after Swann's death. His primary role in *Du Côté de che Swann* is the manner by which Odette uses him to arouse Swann's jealousy. Much later, he adopts Gilberte, giving her an aristocratic name.

THE GUERMANTES CIRCLE

The Prince And Princesse De Guermantes-Baviere: Oriane, Princesse des Laumes, becomes the Princesse de Guermantes. The Guermantes name represents the epitome of oldline aristocracy whose ancestry dating back to Genevieve de Brabant of the Merovingean Age is commemorated in the church of Saint-Hilaire in Combray. Their pathway, the "Guermantes Way," extends from Aunt Léonie's Combray estate along the countryside bordering the Vivonne River. Eventually, the aggressive Mme. Verdurin becomes the titled Princesse through marriage, as the aristocracy falls into its final throes of impotence and money-consciousness.

The Duc And Duchesse De Guermantes: Basin, Prince des Laumes, becomes the Duc de Guermantes but does not figure as prominently in the cycle as the Duchesse. Proust depicts them as incurable snobs, characterizing them also by obsessive attractions to social inferiors. This trait becomes increasingly accentuated as the Duchesse grows older. However, the primary role of the Duchesse is the effect she has upon Marcel as a boy and young adolescent. In youth, Marcel envisioned the Duchesse idealistically in his reveries, evoking her beauty and the mystery of French Merovingean history and legend. He was enthralled by the vision of the Duchesse in the little Combray church in *Du Côté de chez Swann (Swann's Way)*, but once he came actually to meet her and be presented to her socially in *Le Côté de Guermantes (The Guermantes Way)*, the idealized childhood vision vanishes - and the Duchesse emerges merely as another shrewd, coldly calculating woman.

Palamède, Baron De Charlus: the younger brother of Basin, Duc de Guermantes and brother of Mme. de Mersantes. He is the cousin and brother-in-law of the Duchesse, and is the nephew of Robert de Saint Loup and the condescending Mme. de Villeparisis. The Baron de Charlus first appears as a harmless middle-aged man who is trusted in the company of Odette and Gilberte at Swann's Tansonville, but emerges by *Sodome et Gomorrhe (Cities of the Plain)* as an accursed, arrogant snob. His plunge to pathetic destruction is recounted in the latter volumes of the cycle, culminating in *Le Temps retrouvé (The Past Recaptured)*. De Charlus' mismatched inter-class relationship with Morel bears the same earmarks of jealousy as those of Swann with Odette, and of Marcel with Gilberte and Albertine. As an insanely proud aristocrat, de Charlus is ardently anti-Dreyfus and ultimately becomes pro-German. Marcel is later to observe the Baron in much the same way as he did Mlle. Vinteuil.

Marquis Robert De Saint Loup En Bray: son of Aynard and Marie de Mersantes (sister to the Duc); nephew of Mme. de

Villeparisis and of the Baron de Charlus. Marcel becomes the close friend of Saint Loup through Mme. de Villeparisis and visits him at Doncières. As a snob, he selects his friends from among his social inferiors as is the case with the Jewish actress Rachel. After his marriage to Gilberte, we become aware of his weak masochistic side, but we know him also as a war hero. He dies in the front lines and his obituary moves us. Interestingly, even though Saint Loup is an aristocrat, he is a pro-Dreyfusard.

Mme. De Villeparisis: the aunt of Robert de Saint Loup, and an old convent schoolfriend of Marcel's grandmother's. It is through the renewal of that early friendship that Marcel became acquainted with Robert de Saint Loup at the Balbec sea resort. She is a mistress of M. de Norpois for which she suffers social scorn, but she is still associated with the aristocracy and conducts herself in a snobbish condescending manner.

Mme. De Saint-Euverte: a lower aristocrat at whose salon Proust develops the "little phrase" **theme** at a musicale which Swann attends in "Un Amour de Swann." The **imagery** in the Saint-Euverte entertainment sequence is unsurpassed.

A significant cluster of characters in *À la Recherche du temps perdu (Remembrance of Things Past)* are peripheral characters from low life who surround the Guermantes circle and ultimately penetrate it through such universal human equalizers as love or vice. Among these we find the actress Rachel whom Marcel recalls having glimpsed in a house of ill-fame while with Bloch, yet who becomes involved with the aristocratic Robert de Saint Loup. We also find Jupien, the tailor of the Guermantes, in the company of the Baron de Charlus. Likewise, we later find Morel in a deeply psychological and socially mismatched relationship with the Baron.

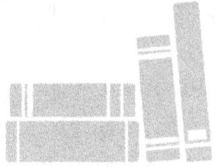

REMEMBRANCE OF THINGS PAST

PROUSTIAN ARTIST-FIGURE AS A FORGOTTEN MAN

....

It is of paramount significance in Proust's *À la Recherche du temps perdu (Remembrance of Things Past)* that, as the mundane world of society seems headed into Dostoevskian chaos, the artist-redeemers seem also to be overlooked and forgotten by common, ordinary men. As precious moments elude us until retrieved by the saving force of redemptive involuntary memory, likewise, the great minds of the time elude the ordinary consciousness. Elstir is overlooked, even regarded as crude while serving under Mme. Verdurin, but is subsequently discovered as possessing great artistic talent. In the interpretation of misty seascapes, he discovers his metaphorical identity and becomes an artist of great stature. Vinteuil is also unknown and unacclaimed, but is even more striking than Elstir for the musician's life is a tragedy. It is only after his death that he rises to heights in public acclaim, and it is ironically through the efforts of his beloved daughter's accomplice in vice and paternal profanation. M. Vinteuil's life reminds us of that of Cesar Auguste Franck (1822-1890), whose *Sonata for Piano and Violin* (1886) resembles the Vinteuil Sonata with its Franck-like recurring motifs, and whose work received negligible appreciation during the composer's lifetime. The Belgian-French Franck also utilized classical forms in deeply mystical, brooding, and emotional cyclical phraseology which seems to bear kinship to the seven notes of Vinteuil's sadly haunting "little phrase."

The actress La Berma, who eventually ascends to fame in her interpretations of classical heroines, reminds us of the slowly rising late-to-fame French actress, Sarah Bernhardt (1844-1923). Consistent with the other Proustian artist figures, Bernhardt (of which La Berma is an obvious anagram) made her debut as a classical tragic heroine but attracted little notice until much later in her life. La Berma also reminds us somewhat of Réjane, another prominent French actress.

The most poignant example of a forgotten artist in the Proustian tapestry is that of the Dutch painter of **genre** and landscapes, Johann [or Jan] Vermeer van Delft (1632-1675) with whom Swann and Marcel have obsessions, with whom Bergotte comes to identify metaphorically in death, and to whose almost Impressionistic work Elstir's bears a resemblance. It has been generally conceded that Vermeer's works, especially his "View of Delft" which hangs in The Hague, rank among the rarest and greatest paintings in the Western world. His work, however, was forgotten during the eighteenth century and much of the nineteenth century until interest in Impressionistic art stimulated studies of the Dutchman's works. They were, in fact, attributed to other painters for a time, attesting to the fact that the master Vermeer was truly a forgotten man. Further comment on the "View of Delft" appears in later portions of this study of Proust. A viewing of at least a reproduction of the painting, preferably one in color (few such seem to be available), is imperative in the full enjoyment of Elstir's work and of the characters' reactions to Vermeer's.

There are **allusions** to scores of other artists in nearly all disciplines in *À la Recherche du temps perdu (Remembrance of Things Past)* but it would suffice at this point to simply refer the reader to the encyclopedias, P. A. Spalding's *A Reader's Handbook to Proust*, and the annotated French Pléiade edition of the entire novel cycle. Perhaps the one other painter who could be considered as warranting comment at this point is another Dutch genre painter in the seventeenth-century vintage and idiom of Vermeer - Pieter de Hooch (1629-after 1677). Proust alludes to sunlight effects falling upon persons amid domestic interior settings glowing in yellow or gold in the manner of a de Hooch painting. The balance, charm, and harmony of such passages is enhanced by a cursory familiarity with the artists alluded to by Proust.

MARCEL PROUST

ANALYSIS OF PROUST'S STYLE

The secret of Proust's style lies in his conception of **metaphor** as being not just a technique but a vision. As a writer, his basic principle of literary creation lay in the "phrase types," the writer's counterpart to the "little phrase" **metaphor** of Vinteuil and the ambiguous Impressionistic **metaphor** of Elstir. Proust himself wrote that for the writer, style was not just a matter of technique but one of vision. In terms of **metaphor** wherein style and vision interact, Proust wrote masterfully in *À l'Ombre des jeunes filles en fleurs (Within a Budding Grove)* upon Elstir's seascapes that their magical appeal lay in "...un sorte de métamorphose...analogue à celle qu'en poésie on nomme métaphore..." (I:835), "...a kind of metamorphosis...analogous to what we call **metaphor** in poetry... "Elstir's secret of metaphorical blending gives his work its ambiguity of land and sea; he would "...suppremait entre elles toute demarcation..." (I:836) "...supress all demarcation between them..." His creative vision was not to merely reproduce things as we know them in the ordinary sense from having got used to them, but to give them that newness and mystery of things seen for the first time through the uncontaminated "innocent eye" which grasps the initial poetical effect; rather than presenting things as they are known to our tired eyes, but by "...ces illusions optiques dont notre vision première est faîte..." (I:868) "...these optical illusions of which our first glimpse is made..."*

Proust's most masterful expository passage on style appears after the succession of involuntary memory sequences in *Le Temps retrouvé (The Past Recaptured)* wherein he discusses the nature of man's discovery of truth through time **metaphor**. This is possibly the most frequently quoted passage in *À la Recherche du temps perdu*, for it grasps the apprehending of pure Truth by a writer. It is the key to literature and echoes of Baudelaire's "correspondences": "...la verité ne commencera qu'au moment ou l'écrivain prendra deux objects différents...les enfermera dans les anneaux nécessaires d'un beau style; même, ainsi que la vie, quand, en rapprochant une qualité commune a deux sensations, il dégagera leur essence commune en les réunissent l'une et l'autre pour les soustraire aux contingences du temps, dans une métaphore... "(III:889), "...truth will come only at that moment when the writer takes two different objects...encloses them in the necessary couplings of good style; quite so in life too, when we compare a common quality in two sensations, we attain to their common essence in reuniting them to one another, in order that we may liberate them from the contingencies of time in a metaphor..."

Even though Proust was under the influence of Flaubert's "le mot juste" technique, Proust's style bore modifications of traditional form and syntax which transformed it into something quite different from the strict Naturalistic style of the nineteenth century. His **imagery** was to be new and highly original, and even though his sentences were to be long and heavy-laden with subjunctive clauses, they were to contain metaphorical

---

* Quotations by kind permission of Alfred A. Knopf, Inc., and Random House, Inc.
  The translations are originals by this author.

relationships of rare complexity. In a way, his style was to be a perfect blend of Classical memoir writing, Naturalism, and subjective modernity. The **imagery** which one finds in *Du Côté de chez Swann (Swann's Way)* is fabulously rare: it grows like crystal, this crystalline growth-process progressing from an original image like that of the magic lantern to later recurrences in stained glass windows, and massive light-deflection **imagery** in the references to music and place names. There is also a profusion of all sorts of organic **imagery**, ranging from the botanical, the ornithological, and the aquatic, to the zoological.

The finest examples of Proust's metaphorical style as it appears actually at work in the poetically rich *Du Côté de chez Swann* are the synaesthetic metaphorical passages. Remarks have already been made upon the influence of Baudelairean "correspondences" and other Symboliste elements in Proust's use of the language of poetry, but the richest passages are those in which the disparate elements come from different sense realms. A profusion of such **imagery** may be found in the descriptions of Vinteuil's music in the Mme. de Saint-Euverte musicale in "Un Amour de Swann" and in "Place Names: the Name." Included immediately below are several examples of the most exquisite Proustian **imagery** from the musicale. One passage suggests how musical contours follow spatial lines and even draw little designs. The notes go along by "...leur hauteur et leur quantité, a couvrir...des surfaces de dimensions variées, a tracer des arabesques..." (I:209), "...their reach and their volume, to cover... surfaces of different dimensions, to draw arabesque patterns..." Another passage which also focuses on the Vinteuil "little phrase," the metaphorical "phrase type" of the musical world, interprets sound not just in terms of Gestalt configurations and complex intersecting designs, but actually transcends the linear realm by its effects with color. It is likened to "...une bulle irisée qui se soutient...un arc-de-ciel... aux couleurs qu'elle avait jusque-la laisse paraitre, elle ajouta d'autres cordes diaprées, toutes celles du prisme." (I:352) The phrase reminds one of "...a suspended iridescent bubble...a rainbow...to the colors it had until then revealed, it added to the others chords struck with all the colors of the prism..."

In addition to the superlative synaesthesia rendered to the Vinteuil phrase, Proust also personifies selections of music in terms of various animate creatures. One of the most memorable passages of this type appears also in the musicale sequence alluded to above, and likens an agile piano selection of Chopin to fabulous tame birds capable of lofty graceful flight. It suggests that one Mme. Franquetot had been brought up to literally caress the notes of the pianist-composer: "....caresser les phrases, au long col sinueux et démesuré...si libres, si flexibles, si tactiles..." (I:331), "...to caress those phrases with the long, sinuous, free-flowing necks...so liberated, so flexible, so tactile..."

There are many beautiful passages in Proust involving various sorts of flowers, but among the most memorable is one describing the passing by of lilacs at the end of their short blossoming time. This passage, like the previous one describing the notes of Chopin, is brilliantly translated by Charles Kenneth Scott-Moncrieff and no attempt by a purely academic commentator could even be compared to the Scotsman's, but the student can nevertheless draw immense joy from it in Proust's original French. It suggests that a few lilacs still remain, but that the majority have gone by even though just one short week before they had been at their height. Now they are like hollow shells: "...leur mousse embaumée, se flétrissait, diminuée et noircie, une écume creuse..." (I:136), "...their fragrant froth, became bespoilt, shrunken up and turning brown, asunken in scum..."

Finally, among the most delightful of the image-laden passages, are those projecting the young and innocent Marcel's imaginary visions evoked by the place names which appear on railroad timetables. Some of the places whose names fascinate him are those which appear along the local line to Balbec, which the train passed each day at exactly one twenty-two. Some of the places are further away, like Parma, which seems "...compact, lisse, mauve et doux..." (I:388), "...compact, smooth, purplish and soft..." Bayeux also holds a fascination "...si haute dans sa noble dentelle rougeâtre et dont le faîte était illuminé par le vieil or de sa dernière syllable..." (I:388-9), "...so statuesque in its noble reddish lace of which its tallest point was illuminéd by the antique gold of its last syllable..." And there was Coutances, a "cathédrale normande, que sa diphtongue finale, grasse et jaunissante, couronne par un tour de buerre..." (I:388-9), "a Norman cathedral of which the rich and yellowing final diphthong is crowned by a tower of butter." These metaphorically enlivened names capture the essence of the child's imagination as they also prepare us for the disillusionments of place realities like Balbec with its Persian church. One could also embark on a metaphorical study of the poetical involuntary memory sequences, but with an understanding of the basics of Proustian **metaphor** and Baudelairean "correspondences," the student will be able to examine the **metaphor** of each involuntary memory sequence upon looking up each from the index provided.

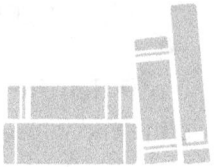

MARCEL PROUST

THEME OF HIDDEN VICE: BIBLICAL ROOTS AND ITS EMERGENCE IN MODERN LITERATURE

Throughout mankind's existence, the subject of homosexuality has been one meeting a great amount of abhorrence and revulsion, and this attitude prevails for the most part today as well. Since early Biblical times, dating from the Scripture recorded in the Book of Genesis, male and female homosexuality have been the most accursed of vices, drawing their nomenclature from Sodom and Gomorrah, the two cities of the plain destroyed in Jehovah's fury by fire and brimstone. The names of the two cities often fill people with disgust, and it is often the victim of the vice itself who experiences the greatest shame and aversion toward it. Many, as psychiatrists today tell us, are only latent victims but nevertheless keep their psychological condition enshrouded in darkest secrecy. It is believed that Proust himself fell in this category, for his tastes ran along lines considered by many to be too feminine to be considered normal or acceptable in the everyday world. Some biographers are, however, far more committal and harsh toward Proust in terms of alleged homosexuality than others. Richard Barker is probably the one who alleges it the most assertively. Allegations of this sort may or may not be entirely justified, however, for Proust's entire life was one which departed from the norm. It is true that he had somewhat feminine tastes which included frequenting the cultural salons, admiring flowers, and general leanings toward artistic things. These, as well as his physical delicacy, were most likely brought upon Proust by his ill health, and there is no truly solid, air-tight evidence in the form of records stating that Proust was psychologically projecting his own self in characters like Morel, Jupien, and the Baron de Charlus.

Proust treats the subject of homosexuality with a singular horror: the sheer volume of his chilling section on this subject is testimony to this - not to mention the haunting, cryptic, image-laden prose he utilizes. Most significantly, he seemed not to dare to write upon this forbidden world until he fell into the despondent state of mind following his parents' deaths. Many critics, in fact, dismiss *Sodom et Gomorrhe (Cities of the Plain)* as precisely the work of a terminally ill and discouraged man. Proust's affection for his parents, especially his mother, was great - and it is generally agreed that he did avoid writing much of the material while they were living to avoid bringing shock and suspicion to them. The above-mentioned thoughts and events had much to do with the growth of *À la Recherche du temps perdu (Remembrance of Things Past)* into a seven-novel work. The abyss in the center, however, reminds us of the nether hell and purgatory of Dante's *Divina Commedia*, and it serves ultimately in the perfection of the triad of life, death, and redemption in Proust.

Proust's material on the feminine-man and the masculine-woman is handled with a Biblical fervor, not the blase acceptance of later writers like the nevertheless-brilliant Andre Gide. Proust's heavy **allusion** to the Old Testament gives his work an Anglo-Saxon quality, and one can readily observe that his affinity to Anglo-Saxonism was profound. Proust is, nevertheless, compassionate toward the vice-ridden for he presents them as deterministic and pathetic creatures in a world churning through irreconcilible change manifest in "déclassement," an Industrial Revolution, and a Great War. Proust's world seems reminiscent of the one of which Dostoevski wrote a generation before, on the other side of Germany: it is a world headed toward a plunge into chaos, and so the element of ambiguity of gender merely serves as part of that vast Proustian pattern preparing us for the ultimate transfiguration of the artist.

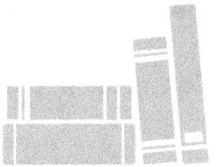

MARCEL PROUST

TRANSLATION OF PROUST INTO ENGLISH

It was in the September 21, 1922 edition of the *London Times Literary Supplement* that the first review of Charles Kenneth Scott-Moncrieff's translation of Proust appeared. C. K. Scott-Moncrieff's *Swann's Way* appeared in 1923, published by Chatto and Windus of London, whom he had persuaded to print his English translations of the seven-novel cycle. Immediately before Proust's death, the French author who knew so little of the English language but who loved Anglo-Saxon literature, was unimpressed by C.K. Scott-Moncrieff's title for the cycle, *Remembrance of Things Past*. Proust, being unfamiliar with the Shakespearean sonnets, unfortunately was not attuned to the depth and subtle nuance of the English title. Proust had hoped for a much more literal translation of *À la Recherche du temps perdu*, seeking a counterbalancing symmetrical title to fit against the final novel's title, *Le Temps retrouvé*. One may draw a full appreciation for Scott-Moncrieff's title upon referring to William Shakespeare's **Sonnet XXX**, with its lingering lamenting quality of form and content and its use of that superlative seventeenth-century English that Scott-Moncrieff loved so well, not only in Shakespeare, but in the King James Bible too:

> When to the sessions of sweet silent thought
>
> I summon up remembrance of things past,
>
> I sigh the lack of many things I sought;
>
> And with old woes new wail my dear time's waste:
>
> Then can I drown an eye unused to flow,
>
> For precious friends hid in death's dateless night,
>
> And weep afresh love's long since concealed woe,
>
> And moan the expense of many a vanished sight:
>
> Then can I grieve at grievances foregone;
>
> And heavily from woe to woe tell o'er
>
> The sad account of fore bemoaned moan,
>
> Which I new pay as if not paid before.
>
> But if the while I think on thee, dear friend,
>
> All losses are restored and losses end.

The time-imbued sense of disillusionment, loss, and isolation is heavy in **Sonnet XXX**, giving it a quality appropriate to a translation of that "temps perdu" for which we are destined to search. Proust's resolution - his "thee, dear friend" - is that one realm which remains intact despite "my dear time's waste" amid "death's dateless night," and the flux imbued sadness of "many a vanished sight." The world of art and its discovery through metaphor assures the narrator that "All losses are restored and losses end."

Charles Kenneth Scott-Moncrieff was a translator of not only Marcel Proust, but of Luigi Pirandello and Henri (Beyle) Stendhal. Through his imaginatively masterful craftsmanship with the English language, he (along with Constance Garnett, the English translator of Fyodor Dostoevski) raised the status of the translator from one of midwifery to one of family status, the translator's work joining with and contributing to the lineage of the complete work. Scott-Moncrieff did more than translate: he added new dimension to a work.

Proust's style is an intricate grammatical structure involving profuse numbers of subjunctive clauses which are difficult to translate into English. The result is frequently a translated passage laden with auxiliary verbs and no readily distinguishable subjunctive mood. Proust also frequently used the highly concentrated imperfect tense (which translates as "would do" although the tense itself can be created through auxiliary verb or "used to do" in English). Its compact melancholia and sadness of inflection is untranslatable from French into English - formations which frequently become overly dilute and prolix. Such complex French as that in À la Recherche du temps perdu calls for an extremely competent translator.

Despite the impossibility of reproducing the uvular fragrances of poetic French in English, the dark reverberations of C. K. Scott-Moncrieff's Renaissance-Victorian English have an elusiveness that is unique to the Germanic languages, giving the complexities of sentence structure a languid, unrigid quality. French, the language of "scientisme" and the traditional international language of diplomacy, is more explicit and idiomatically exact than the mysterious but beautifully ambiguous English. Scott-Moncrieff's mastery of Proust is confirmed by the fact that he did not attempt to translate his work literally. Rather, he translated obliquely and allusively - a method perfectly suited to the cycle of novels which are themselves thickly allusive. His titles within the cycle are masterpieces. Because the word "côté" can mean "way" as in a way of life, as well as meaning "side," Scott-Moncrieff was able to derive *Swann's Way* and *The Guermantes Way* with great ease. In his translation of *Sodome et Gomorrhe*, by using a parenthetical **allusion** to those same two doomed cities from the King James Book of Genesis, he derived his subtly oblique but impeccably accurate *Cities of the Plain*. The words *The Captive* are much more abstract and less discursive than the more obvious "prisoner" and bear more of the psychological weight of inner captivity. *The Past Recaptured* is sublime in its liberation from the fetters of any attempt at literal translation, as is the assonant and consonant *The Sweet Cheat Gone* from Walter de la Mare's poem, and the iambic *Within A Budding Grove*.

One of the most exemplary passages of Charles Kenneth Scott-Moncrieff is his translation of the passage from *Swann's Way* describing the withering away of bygone lilacs alluded to in the section on Proust's style. He translates the word for "overflowed" ("effusaient") superbly as "thrust aloft," and he translates the rather strong verb "se flétrissait" which suggests spoilage and besmirching, quite gently but with muted effectiveness as "discoloured." Because "déferlait" means "burst out in foam," the translator sustains the watery **imagery** in his translation of "écume" as "scum." The trochaic downward inflection of "hollow, scentless scum" gives the material a sad beauty and a rare music. The reference to their previously having been "breaking in waves of fragrant foam" counterbalances "scum" perfectly as far as **consonance** is concerned, but more perfectly in the subtle formation of a **metaphor** by describing flowers in terms of the sea and suppressing the line of demarcation between the two. The polarization of the life-bearing "foam" against the ugly "scum" brings the whole passage into play in its anticipation of the even more ugly Montjouvain scene.

Another superlative passage of Proust's English translator is that describing the phrases of Chopin alluded to earlier in terms of its French original. Scott-Moncrieff has added to the beauty of the French passage by altering it slightly but subtly in English. Rather than just translating "caresser" as merely "caress," he gives the passage a redolence and warmth by translating the one verb into "fondle and cherish." Also, rather than just retaining the basic idea that the phrases of Chopin have long necks, he actually animates the passage by the addition of the soft trochee, "creatures," giving the word "phrases" just parenthetical status. The word "creatures" becomes the object of the double verb and bears tremendous metaphorical impact. So the passage reads: "...to fondle and cherish those long necked, sinuous creatures..." The passage is effective in its suggestive quality as to the demands of Chopin's music upon the long, sinuous, flexible fingers of a concert pianist.

Charles Kenneth Scott-Moncrieff was born on September 25, 1889 in Sterlingshire, Scotland and received his education at Inverness College, Winchester, and Edinburgh University. He worked for the *London Times* from 1921 to 1923 and was subsequently commissioned by Chatto and Windus to translate Marcel Proust's *À la Recherche du temps perdu*. He pursued this enormous task to his last years of illness which was rooted to injury and fever sustained during World War I. He spent his final years in Italy, moving from Pisa to Rome in 1927 where he edited proofs of *The Sweet Cheat Gone* before his early death at age 40 on February 28, 1930 at a nursing home. (In Kunitz's *Twentieth*

Century Authors (H. W. Wilson, Co., 1942) the Scotsman's last name is hyphenated and appears under "S," although some publishers seem to be at variance over this finer point.) C. K. Scott-Moncrieff, unfortunately, did not live to translate *Le Temps retrouvé'* - for the craftsmanship of Scott-Moncrieff's successor, Frederick Blossom, is dwarfed by the masterful prose of the original translator. Since that time, Stephen Hudson, and more recently, Andreas Mayor, have undertaken the project of translating *Le Temps retrouvé*. The finished Mayor translation of the final novel ranks with Scott-Moncrieff's translation of the others and is regarded as the authentic synthesized translation of the heretofore unfinished and fragmentary last novel. The exhaustive efforts at restoring *Le Temps retrouvé'* in the chronological perspective of the other novels have made the seventh novel more coherent to the reader.

Marcel Proust as a Critic: Proust is considered a novelist by most readers because most of his critical work is regarded as preparatory to *À la Recherche du temps perdu* and is thereby eclipsed by the novel cycle. He was, however, a literary critic of a high order and, like D. H. Lawrence and Henry James, was a critic-novelist of the first order. Proust's criticism is an integral part of his fictional technique, for his grasp of the technique and mentality of his neo-Classical, Romantic, and Realist-Naturalist predecessors surfaces in the critical **exposition** and parodies of *Pastiches et Mélanges* and in the characterizations and prose technique of *À la Recherche du temps perdu*. Criticism in *À la Recherche du temps perdu* shows a particular maturity, for much of it is derived from his own aesthetic experience and analytical formulation.

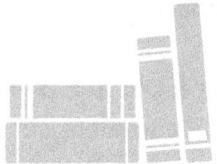

REMEMBRANCE OF THINGS PAST

RECAPITULATION: REMEMBRANCE OF THINGS PAST AS AN ARTISTIC UNITY

In recapitulation, one may take a retrospective glance at the seven-novel cycle as a whole and take notice of certain structural and artistic elements which give the enormous work an aesthetic balance, harmony, and unity. In the progression of the work, one should be observant of many seemingly commonplace events in its chronological unfolding and in various chance occurrences. This is the way motifs and underlying elements evoked by involuntary memory are built. Upon studying these notes, the student should become aware of the most significant recurrences in the artistic structuring of *À la Recherche du temps perdu (Remembrance of Things Past)*.

Chronologically, we move basically from Marcel's recalled childhood in *Du Côté de chez Swann (Swann's Way)* to his adolescence and young manhood in *À l'Ombre des jeunes filles en fleurs (Within a Budding Grove)* where Marcel's love for Gilberte covers nearly a year and a half - beginning in the autumn of one year and continuing through the autumn and winter of another. By the time of Marcel's first summer at Balbec to that following autumn which is signaled at the end of *À l'Ombre des jeunes filles en fleurs*, two full years have passed from the beginning of the Gilberte affair. The complete second novel begins about two years prior to the beginning of the Gilberte affair and ends about six months after its termination - covering in all a span of about four years.

Sodome et Gomorrhe (Cities of the Plain) covers Marcel's first winter on the Parisian Faubourg Saint-Germain, and his retreat to Balbec for a second visit following that winter, comes a full year after Doncières and his grandmother's death.

It is that autumn after the second summer at Balbec that Albertine comes to stay for a full year with Marcel. This central sector of the novel cycle consists of four closely related novels which follow one another in rapid succession: *Le Côté de Guermantes (The Guermantes Way)*, *Sodome et Gomorrhe (Cities of the Plain)*, *La Prisonnière (The Captive)*, and *Albertine Disparue (The Sweet Cheat Gone)*. In *Le Temps retrouvé (The Past Recaptured)*, which takes us to wartime Paris - plus a vague post-war period of some sixteen years thereafter - we find Marcel a matured, disillusioned middle-aged man.

It has already been asserted that, despite the random and chance nature of the cycle's growth from its original blueprint as a three-novel work, it was drafted into a seven-novel work with painstaking care and a scrupulous regard for recurring characters, motifs, and incidents. Its artistic unity is sealed airtight by the triadic rhythm of the life-death-resurrection thematology and by parallel structure between the seven-novel tier structure and that of the elusive seven-note phrase which serves as the basis for the "phrase types."

Not only do the basic three- and seven-part structures of the novel itself give it artistic unity, but the consistency of the mismatched love-jealousy-disillusionment pattern which has been discussed at length heretofore also serves to unify the work. The underpinning of the two "ways" serves also to give way to another "way" - that of art as the other two formerly exclusive ways coalesce - resolving the thematic contingent relating to the society-"snobisme" syndrome.

Serving otherwise to unify the work are the important symbols and motifs which sustain the important **themes** of the cycle. Among these is the symbol of autumn, suggestive of the relentlessness of cyclical time. Another is that of the little tinkling gate-bell which appears at both the beginning and the end of the cycle, suggestive at the end of a rebirth of the Combray in which it was originally heard by Marcel as a child awaiting the departure of Swann. As in the Mass, the bell seems to suggest a consecration, that of the filial love between Marcel and his mother, consummated in the tenderness of the goodnight kiss. It signals at the end, along with the recurrence of François le Champi, the consecration of Marcel's vocation as an artist. Another of the most prominent unifying elements appearing at both ends of the novel cycle is the recurrence of the word "temps."

The artist figures, of course, serve to unify the cycle - for even though their language or medium differs in each case - the basic metaphorical vision is interdisciplinary and transcends the limitations of form. The **allusions** to the various arts, which run in the hundreds throughout *À la Recherche du temps perdu*, become amalgamated when the various arts are perceived through the consciousness of a Swann or more significantly a Marcel.

The various locations in which the enormous novel cycle is set are also brought together by the artist figures: Combray by

Vinteuil, Balbec by Elstir, and Paris by La Berma and Bergotte. The persistent strain of Vinteuil weaves the thread of Combray through the entire work to its end when we hear part of the Septet at the matinee of the Princesse de Guermantes. Venice, likewise, is associated with the art and architecture of the brilliant Italian Renaissance which is embodied in St. Mark's Cathedral. Of the individual works of art alluded to in the cycle, the most significant of the paintings is Vermeer's "View of Delft" which seems to assert a thwarted sense of the illusory in Bergotte's own work - artistically incomplete for oversight of what might seem commonplace but in actuality it is metaphorically sublime.

In concluding the recapitulation of *À la Recherche du temps perdu* in terms of its artistic unity, it bears mentioning that perhaps the most consistent strain of **metaphor** throughout the novel cycle is that linking and resolving disparate moments in time with their inter-sensory responses or "correspondences." A list of the twenty-two such moments follows with page references to the new Vintage paperback editions in English, and to the complete three-volume Pléiade edition in French. The Vintage English titles are initialed and the French volumes are referred to by volume number.

1. Tea-Madeleine: VSW: 33-36/I: 44-48

2. Steeples of Martinville: VSW: 137-40/I: 178-82

3. Pavilion in Champs-Élysées: VWBG: 49-50/I: 491-94

4. Trees at Hudimesnil: VWBG: 215-6/I: 717-19

5. Flowerless hawthorns near Balbec: VWBG: 362/: 922

6. Radiator gurgle at Doncières: VGW: 250-1/II: 347-8

7. Memory with Saint Loup in Paris: VGW: 286-7/II: 396-8

8. After Dinner at the Duc de Guermantes: VGW: 390-1/II: 547-9

9. Unbuttoning boots-Grand Hôtel at Balbec: VCP: 113-7/II: 755-60

10. Twigs burning: VC: 15-16/III: 26-7

11. Onset of Cold Weather: VC: 38-39/III: 58-9

12. Septet of Vinteuil: VC: 178-183/III: 248-65

13. Smell of Gasoline: VC: 286-7/III: 411-12

14. Rain and the gurgle of a radiator: VSCG: 55-8/III: 490-4

15. Touch of Scarf: VSCG: 83-4/III: 531-2

16. Train stop in open country: VPR: 120-1/III: 854-56

17. Streets near Guermantes' Mansion: VPR: 123-/III: 858

18. Uneven Flagstones-Venice: VPR: 129-30/III: 866-7

19. Spoon-plate recalling hammer on wheel: VPR: 130/III: 868

20. Starched napkin-Balbec blue: VPR: 131/III: 868

21. Gurgle in pipe: VPR: 135/III: 874

22. François le Champi: VPR: 142-3/III: 883-86

ESSAY QUESTIONS AND ANSWERS

Upon studying this book, the well prepared student should be able to anticipate stock questions regarding the basic structural elements of the cycle, the character mutations, and the moments of heightened awareness. As preparation, therefore, the student may easily extrapolate anticipated examination answers from the various segments on the separate novels, the influences, and the biographical overtones. Repeating the same material as has appeared earlier would be unnecessary, so the selected examination questions will concern themselves with variations and extensions of material already introduced. Most examiners in undergraduate courses will ask questions relating to Du Côté de chez Swann (Swann's Way). Graduate credit courses frequently cover some or all of the other novels of the cycle.

Question: Discuss the roles of M. Swann and Marcel as projections of Proust himself, focusing primarily on *Du Côté de chez Swann (Swann's Way)*.

Answer: One may find projections of various facets of Marcel Proust's personality in any number of the characters in *Du Côté de chez Swann* as well as in the rest of the cycle, such as in the case of Bergotte at the Vermeer exhibition in *La Prisonnière (The Captive)*. One can take particular notice, however, of the Proust element in Swann and Marcel in *Du Côté de chez Swann (Swann's Way)* and in Marcel in *Le Temps retrouvé (The Past Recaptured)*. Even though Charles Swann is a generation older than Marcel, he basically represents the young and worldly Proust of the early years before the claustrophobic confinement inflicted upon him by his chronic asthma. Swann, like Proust, has a vision whereby all is seen in terms of some famous work of art, and he has embryonic ideas of writing a monograph on Vermeer which he never fulfills on account of preoccupation with society. Swann serves as a kind of artistic mentor for Marcel in matters of taste and envisions Odette in terms of Botticelli's rendering of Zipporah, Jethro's daughter, in a fresco at the Sistine Chapel. He sees Bloch in terms of Mohamet II, and sees rooms in terms of De Hooch's paintings of Dutch sunlit interiors. Swann also bears a similarity to Proust himself in his Jewish strain and in his comfortable financial position.

Marcel, under the tutelage of Swann and his culturally inclined mother, reminds us of Proust himself in his preoccupation with the deeper philosophical aspects of art. He is a projection of the older, more mature Proust - the Proust of lost childhood, disillusionment, asthma, and artistic revelation and salvation. Marcel, like the secluded Proust, looks back to his childhood in an idyllic French town with an affectionate and devoted mother. Some may even believe that there are Oedipal overtones in Marcel's overwrought and obsessive jealousy over his mother, for the motif of the prolonged and anguished wait for her kiss recurs at powerful strategic points over the course of the entire novel cycle. Marcel, like the maturing Proust, took an outsider's view of the banalities of social climbing, sifting them through his own memoirist's consciousness. The resurrection sequence relating to the writer's vocation, and the expository analysis in the Guermantes' library project Proust's own artistic theory in *Le Temps retrouvé (The Past Recaptured)* as does the **exposition** on Elstir's paintings relating his conception of **metaphor** in *À l'Ombre des jeunes filles en fleurs (Within a Budding Grove)*.

Question: Discuss in existential terms the problems of identity in Marcel's life in the cycle. (This question is very broad, but its answer-nucleus might serve the student well in the preparation of an independent project.)

Answer: There are specific incidents in the cycle where Marcel expects to identify with a person or place in a certain way, but fails, through an accident of circumstance or a quirk of intuition upon experiencing a particular sensation, to make the anticipated familiar connection. The moments of realization that he has not interacted with an object in the expected way are terrifying to him and contribute to his feeling of the world's lack of preestablished purpose of harmony - its absurdity. Four such instances occur in Marcel's relationship with his grandmother. One is the occurrence when her expected familiar voice takes on a strangely disembodied and transcendent quality over the telephone. Another takes place when he suddenly feels that he does not recognize her when he catches her off guard upon his unannounced arrival home from Doncières. A third, which also takes place in *À l'Ombre des jeunes filles en fleurs (Within a Budding Grove)* like the other two, is that strangely terrifying walk through the Champs-Élysées when the grandmother seems suddenly to be walking strangely and covering her stroke-ridden face with the wide brim of her displaced hat. The final such instance before the grandmother's death takes place in *Le Côté de Guermantes (The Guermantes Way)* when Marcel realizes that she does not recognize him.

In *Sodome et Gomorrhe (Cities of the Plain)*, an identity sequence which is highly existential in its impact through defying the rational world of explanations which we can claim as our own through our intelligence, is that intuitive sequence which brings the sudden emergence of the deceased grandmother's presence into Marcel's room in the Grand Hôtel at Balbec. The identity response to this familiar and beloved presence is tormenting, for the immediate realization of the presence being there brings also the immediate counter-realization that it is forever gone. There is that terrible contradiction between "existence" and "néant" - existence and nothingness - survival and annihilation. The word "néant" appears in several places in the cycle, one of the most prominent being that section just prior to Marcel's entering the Guermantes' mansion in *Le Temps retrouvé (The Past Recaptured)*.

One of the purposes of Proust's cycle is to present with full impact the revelation of Truth through art, but to precede that with a full questioning of the meaning of life in a world that seems to propose none. The overly simplistic and often merely man-inspired (rather than divinely inspired) traditional systems (philosophical, theological, moral) seem incapable of resolving the problem of man's quest for the Absolute. Proust suggests that the nature of existence cannot be apprehended by the intelligence. It calls for an awareness of another sort which will transcend the unauthentic quality of banal society and materialism - that flash of intuition which gives us insight to the essential Reality, similar to what the Proust-influenced James Joyce referred to as "epiphany."

Question: Discuss the characters who are portrayed through the technique of "pastiche."

Answer: Pastiche is derived from a form of satirical writing based on mimicry, dating back to the Classical memoirists Saint-Simon and Mme. de Sévigné. This technique is utilized in a **parody** of the Goncourts' style of writing in their Journal in *Le Temps retrouvé (The Past Recaptured)*, as well as in the portrayal of certain characters which include Françoise, M. de Norpois, Dr. Cottard, the Duchesse de Guermantes, and the Baron de Charlus.

Françoise is endowed with an interesting speech pattern and with mannerisms which are rooted in medieval tradition. She is a senior servant of the old pre-"ancien régime" order and is presented contrastively against the younger, less dedicated servants. Her tongue is sharp, being consistent with her dominant role in the household, and her speech is embroidered with the very embodiment of her traditionalism in her affection for the Classical memoirist Mme. de Sévigné.

M. de Norpois is an old-order diplomat whose speech is heavy laden with pomposities and pseudo-intellectualism in literary matters. He is presented in comic "pastiche" as self-contradictory and given to monopolizing conversations by turning the focus back to his own contrived tastes and by his overuse of threadbare cliches.

Dr. Cottard, like most of the rest of the Verdurin clan in the early parts of the cycle, lends himself perfectly to pastiche. Completely consumed by his intellectual pursuits in medical research, he is lost in a purely social situation and reveals it amusingly by his "gauche" habit of continually reverting to that form of humor which draws its material from plays on words - punning.

When we are exposed to the Duchesse as a person and become disappointedly acquainted with her personally, we also become acquainted with her verbal mannerisms. Her primary mode of self-expression is the use of her wit, which we see closely in *Le Côté de Guermantes (The Guermantes Way)*. The same dependence upon wit is also the case in the character of the Baron de Charlus. However, in his case, the satirical spirit of "pastiche" takes on a dark aspect on account of the fact that he is psychologically afflicted. We dread the Baron, but we pity him nevertheless.

Question: Discuss the moral tone of Proust's À la Recherche du temps perdu (Remembrance of Things Past)

Answer: For a novel considered to be the most influential upon world literature in the twentieth century, Proust's *À la Recherche du temps perdu* is highly moralistic. Even though it is not directly religious, it carries a heavy overlay of the Christian life-death-resurrection **theme** and is suffused in the Hebraic Old Testament consciousness of retribution.

Like the original cities of the plain, the depraved chaos-bound world of World War I seems, likewise, to be engulfed in the fire that we see in wartime Paris in *Le Temps retrouvé' (The Past Recaptured)*. The Baron de de Charlus' affliction is handled by the author with compassion but is treated, nevertheless, as a sin - a sin that takes on the fiery quality of medieval depictions of hell when Marcel sees him from a distance engaged in a frightening flagellation scene.

Mlle. Vinteuil, through an obvious consciousness of retribution, seeks to collect and arrange her martyred father's unfinished work in an exorcism of musical toil. Marcel is himself ridden with feelings of guilt and retribution similar to those in one phase of Job's ordeal - when, upon discovering that Albertine knew Mlle. Vinteuil, he believes that he must be receiving punishment for a terrible transgression. He rationalizes his misery by assuming himself guilty in being a vague root cause in his grandmother's death.

The entire *À la Recherche du temps perdu* is suffused in Biblical references and its moralizing quality seems influenced through his Hebraic consciousness plus his general feeling of inadequacy and guilt. The volume of material he devotes to the crumbling, accursed aristocracy is testimony to this.

Question: Discuss the tragedy of Bergotte.

Answer: Bergotte is but one figure in Marcel's life's quest for literary excellence. As a youth, Marcel regarded Bergotte as his favorite living author, but he eventually outgrows his elaborately stylistic although great work. Bergotte is to discover the consummation of artistic maturity too late. Even though his work is brilliant and Marcel views his work as immortal, Bergotte discovers in Vermeer the ultimate in artistic perfection which he will never live to transcribe. This is the tragedy, for the height of his genius will never be fulfilled. Vermeer's strategically located dab of yellow wall links the disparate elements of the "View of Delft" together in consummate tranquility, balance, and harmony. Metaphorical vision transcends style. This death scene in *La Prisonnière (The Captive)* relates Bergotte's discovery of what Elstir has discovered in the ambiguous sealine melting into a misty sky, and what Marcel will discover in *Le Temps retrouvé (The Past Recaptured)* with involuntary memory - **metaphor** - that poetical key to Truth which brings out a complete and unified art suppressing the lines of distinction in a subject's view of objects which gives inferior art its obvious quality. The patch of yellow wall suppresses the disparity between the water, the sky, and the stone buildings. Likewise the literary counterpart, the "phrase type" in the key image, will accomplish the same for the writer. There is a reality in art which transcends the immediacy of its medium of paint or sound - that essential reality behind the language which is unlocked through metaphorical vision.

Question: Discuss *Du Côté de chez Swann (Swann's Way)* as a self-contained artistic unity.

Answer: Even though *Du Côté de chez Swann* is the introductory novel in the cycle of seven long novels, it is a self-contained work which stands by itself as an artistic unity. It is, of course, recommended that all of the novels be read to derive the fullest appreciation of each, but *Du Côté de chez Swann* may also be read profitably by itself.

Artistic unity prevails in the first novel's content as well as in elements of **imagery**, motif, and symbol. (Referral may be made to the section on *Du Côté de chez Swann* for unifying thematic and formal elements.) The content, or story material, of this novel is artistically complete for, in Classical terms, it has a beginning, a middle, and an end. It begins psychologically "in medias res" (in the midst of things), finding the narrator in a mentally hyperactive state in which he is in the process of remembering various bedrooms in different phases of his life. It also has a kind of recognition scene in which, through the tea and madeleine, Marcel comes suddenly to find his childhood identity intact in a resurrected presence of Combray. The little story of Swann and Odette, which psychologically anticipates Marcel's love predicaments, links us to the presence of Swann which Marcel found so upsetting on the night he missed his mother's kiss. Like the "little phrase" of Vinteuil, "Un Amour de Swann" hangs, structurally perfect and artistically intact, like an iridescent bubble. After the reminiscences of Combray and the retrospective Swann novella, the plot line brings us back full circle to a vague sense of the present.

Amid a myriad of recurring characters, *Du Côté de chez Swann (Swann's Way)* introduces nearly all of the main story elements appearing in the succeeding novels of the cycle - love-jealousy, the kiss, society, Vinteuil's music, the presence of Bergotte and Elstir, contemplation of Vermeer by Swann, and the preeminence of metaphor.

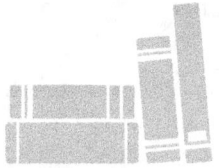

BIBLIOGRAPHY

PRIMARY SOURCES

Proust, Marcel. *À la Recherche du temps perdu Ed.* Pierre Clarac and André Ferre. Bibliothèque de la Pléiade. N. R. F. Editions Gallimard. Paris. 1954.

Proust, Marcel. *Remembrance of Things Past.* Trans. C. K. Scott-Moncrieff. Vintage Editions. Random House. New York.

SECONDARY SOURCES

Barker, Richard H. *Marcel Proust: A Biography.* Criterion. New York. 1958.

Beckett, Samuel. *Proust.* Grove Press. New York. 1957. (This is the U.S. edition of Beckett's book published by Chatto & Windus, London, 1931.)

Bersani, Leo. *Marcel Proust: The Fictions of Life and Art.* Oxford University Press. New York. 1965.

Brée, Germaine. *Marcel Proust and Deliverance from Time.* (Du Temps Perdu au Temps Retrouvé). New Brunswick. Rutgers. 1955. Grove Press, Inc., New York. 1955.)

Brée, Germaine. *The World of Marcel Proust*. Houghton Mifflin Co. Boston. 1966.

Cattaui, Georges. *Marcel Proust*. The Merlin Press Ltd. (Minerva Press) 1967.

Chernowitz, Maurice Eugene. *Proust and Painting*. International University Press. New York. 1944.

Girard, René ed. *Proust. A Collection of Critical Essays*. Prentice-Hall. Englewood Cliffs. New Jersey. 1962.

Green, F. C. *The Min of Proust*. Cambridge University Press. Cambridge. 1949.

Hindus, Milton. *A Reader's Guide to Marcel Proust*. Farrar, Straus and Cudahy. The Noonday Press. 1962.

March, Harold. *The Two Worlds of Marcel Proust*. University of Pennsylvania Press. Philadelphia. 1948.

Maurois, André. *Proust: Portrait of a Genius*. Harper & Bros. (Also published as *Proust: A Biography*. Meridian Books, Inc. New York. 1958.)

Moss, Howard. *The Magic Lantern of Marcel Proust*. Macmillan. New York. 1962.

Painter, George D. *Proust. The Early Years*. Atlantic Monthly Press Book. Little, Brown and Co. Boston. 1959.

Painter, George D. *Proust. The Later Years*. Atlantic Monthly Press Book. Little, Brown and Co. 1965.

Pierre-Quint, Léon. *Marcel Proust, His Life and Work*. Trans. from Marcel Proust, sa vie, son oeuvre. Paris. 1925.

Shattuck, Roger. *Proust's Binoculars: A Study of Memory, Time and Recognition in "À la Recherche du temps perdu."* Vintage Books. Random House. New York. 1963.

Ullman, Stephen. *The Image in the Modern French Novel.* Ch. III. "The Metaphorical Texture of a Proustian Novel." Basil Blackwell. Oxford. 1963.

Virtanen, Reino. "Proust's **Metaphor** from the Natural and Exact Sciences," *PMLA*, Dec. 1954.

Wilson, Edmund. *Axel's Castle: A Study in Imaginative Literature of 1870-1930.* Scribner's. New York. 1953. (pp. 132-190)

www.ingramcontent.com/pod-product-compliance
Lightning Source LLC
LaVergne TN
LVHW011709060526
838200LV00051B/2829